The Doubting Believer

The Doubting Believer

*A Treatise Containing the Nature, the Kinds,
the Springs, and the Remedies of Doubtings
Incident to Weak Believers*

Obadiah Sedgwick

Soli Deo Gloria Publications
An imprint of Reformation Heritage Books
Grand Rapids, Michigan

Soli Deo Gloria Publications
An imprint of Reformation Heritage Books
3070 29th St. SE
Grand Rapids, MI 49512
616-977-0889
orders@heritagebooks.org
www.heritagebooks.org

The Doubting Believer was reprinted in Aberdeen by D. Chalmers in 1819. This Soli Deo Gloria reprint has undergone spelling, grammar, and formatting changes.

Printed in the United States of America
Paperback reprint 2023

ISBN 979-8-88686-008-5

For additional Reformed literature, request a free book list from Reformation Heritage Books at the above regular or e-mail address.

A Table of the Heads In This Treatise

1. Original Sin
2. Imperfection in Faith
3. The Life of Sense
4. Restraining of Faith
5. Special Sins after Conversion
6. Spiritual Indispositions
7. Fruitless Endeavors
8. Imbecility of Judgment
9. Ignorance of the Doctrine of Justification

APPENDIX

The Nature and Danger of Heresies

Dedication

To the Right Honorable
ROBERT,
Earl of Warwick,
Baron of Leez, etc.
My Noble Lord and Free Patron

My Lord,

A renewed heart is a very heaven in our little world, and faith is the only sun in that heaven. The sinner never comes to be precious till he comes to be pious; and the value of that piety still advances according to the quantity of true faith, as the ring is more considerable with the diamond. I cannot conceive of a more compendious way for any Christian's full and constant revenues than this: to get faith, and still to use it; the sum or product of which would be this: grace and glory, heaven and earth are ours.

Satan well knows what a serviceable channel faith is for all our traffic, whether for our ship to launch out into duties or for God's ship to come laden in to us with mercies; and, therefore, there is no grace which he batters and conflicts so with as with faith. If we weaken or shake foundations, this has a spreading influence into the whole building. A Christian's faith cannot be wronged, but presently all the spiritual frame becomes sensible of wrong and loss.

In my weak judgment, it would be a great prudence

to secure that which, being secured, now secures all. Nothing grows weak where faith grows strong. My Lord, this poor treatise, which I presume to front with your name, is like Aaron and Hur, who staid up the hands of Moses. So does this treatise endeavor to stay the hand of faith in a weak believer who has an ample estate on the shore and at land, but those waves of doubtings (when he is thirsting in) too often make him to fall back and stagger. Whence follows this great unhappiness that, whereas his faith might have served in many precious comforts, it is (almost a whole life) employed only to answer fears and doubts. I humbly present the subsequent work to your Lordship's personal use and public patronage. Be pleased (at your leisure) to peruse it and regard it as the first cognizance of my thankfulness to your honor for the living which you so freely and lovingly conferred on me, wherein I shall desire faithfully to serve your Lord and mine.

Now, the Almighty God and blessed Father abundantly enrich your noble heart with all saving graces, and continue you long to be an instrument of much glory to Himself, comfort to His Church, and good to our commonwealth.

Your Honor's Perpetually Obliged,

Obadiah Sedgwick

To The Christian Reader

This treatise, which is now presented to a public construction, was (many years past) the subject of my private meditations and sermons. I did not affect any further publication of it than in the pulpit; but the importunity of others has compelled it thus to appear in print. Not that the manner of handling the subject (here insisted on) is excellent or exquisite, but that the matter handled may be supposed to be of common use and benefit; as a little star has influence, though not that glory which is proper to the sun.

The case which is here put and discussed is a case of common experience. There is no believer but some time or other will confess it is his. The sun being seated in an heavenly orb shines with a very pure and constant light, but the candle, though set and burning in a golden candlestick, yet burns with a snuff and much variableness. When Christians are translated and transplanted from earth to heaven, then their graces shall become perfections. There are no defects in heaven; there are no mixtures in heaven, but whatsoever is pure there is altogether pure. Yet on earth it is otherwise. Neither the habits of grace nor the acts of grace are alone in any Christian. *When I would do good, evil is present with me,* said Paul, and *I believe; Lord, help my unbelief,* said that poor man in the Gospel.

Where is the believer who insists not more on his fears than on his faith and is not lamenting his doubts more often than rejoicing in his assurances? None have an interest in Christ but believers; none have title to a solid and settled peace but they, and yet we see the children fearful and bondmen confident. The best of men still in suit, and the worst of men quiet, as if in full possession, none doubting less than such as have most cause to doubt, and none doubting more than such as have most cause to triumph in Christ. And in truth thus it will be while gross ignorance veils over presumptuous sinners, and misbelief is incident to tender spirits.

And is not the hand of Joab in this business too? Is not Satan in all the sins of wicked men and in most of the troubles of good men? Either he tempts us to sin and that will cause us to doubt, or else he tempts us to doubt and that will cause us to sin. Surely it is not the shortest of his wiles and arts, in matters of religion, to keep the judgments of some still staggering; and, in matters of a soul's interest in Christ, to keep the heart still doubting. Does he not know that the Christian cannot so happily improve Christ, who is still in suit to prove his title to Christ?

For the better expediting of these soul suits, peruse (if you please) this ensuing work, which is (I confess) not a garden for every one to walk in, but only medicine for the sick or weak. It is intended as a hospital for the lame, only for a troubled sinner, only for a weak believer. And the Father of our Lord Jesus Christ, the Father of mercies and the God of all comfort, even He who establishes us in Christ, prosper it for His glory, and the help of some one or other.

Thy Faith's Servant,

Obadiah Sedgwick

A TREATISE OF DOUBTINGS

(From Matthew 14:31)
O thou of little faith, wherefore didst thou doubt?

These words contain in them the sum of a Christian in this life, which is this: that he is truly but yet weakly good. Christ here sees in Peter (though a disciple) a defective faith, and then a defect of faith. Faith He saw in him, yet it was defective. It was little faith. There was truth, but there was not such actual strength in it as might or should be. And, besides this, He sees in him a defect of faith; not for the habit of it, but for the act of it, *Wherefore didst thou doubt?* These words are a conviction that he doubted, and, likewise, a correction, *Wherefore didst thou doubt?* In other words, "You doubted, but you did ill so to doubt."

There are many excellent points which might be observed from the text. I will name some and insist only on one of them. Thus, then:

1. A true believer may be but a weak believer, *Thou of little faith!*
2. Christ takes notice even of a weak believer, *O thou of little faith!*
3. Though Christ likes believing, yet he dislikes doubting, *Wherefore didst thou doubt?*
4. A person may be truly believing who, neverthe less, is sometimes doubting. In the same person here you see a commendation of the one and a

condemnation of the other, which suppose necessarily a presence of both.

This being the subject on which I propose to treat, for the benefit of weak Christians, I shall declare five things concerning it. Namely:

1. The nature of doubtings.
2. The kinds and diversities of them.
3. Their possible consistence with true faith.
4. Their grounds, and springs, and occasions.
5. Their cures and remedies.

Chapter 1

THE NATURE OF DOUBTINGS

To understand this, you must know that in the worst part of the soul, there are several qualities, viz.:

1. Infidelity, which strictly, and among those who profess the Gospel, is a positive reflecting of heavenly truths with their secret goodness. Herein men forsake their own mercies by plain dissents and slightings of the good word of grace, as is evident in the Pharisees, Luke 7:30, who rejected the counsel of God, etc.

2. Despair, which is a manifest dissent, not so much in respect of the thing or object (for this is assented unto us as true in respect of itself, viz. that God is merciful, and Christ died for sinners), but in respect of the person or subject, wherein the soul gives up itself as lost, as without the compass and hopefulness of the divine proclamation. It is persuaded that there is no possibility for it to recover the shore and, therefore, sinks in the depths. My meaning is that such a soul, though it sees that in God, and that in Christ, which can save, and does save others, yet cuts off itself as not at all capable of any interest in the mercy of God or blood of Christ, and so eternally falls under its own weight, as is evident in Judas and Cain.

Now despair, so far as it makes assent unto truths, is opposed unto infidelity; and so far as it dissents from special goodness in them, it is opposed to faith; and so far as it concludes impossibility of that good unto itself, it is opposed to hope.

3. Fearful opinions, which are positive assents unto truths, yet raised upon such probable inducements only, that the soul is left with a suspicion that the contrary may be true, are like a man upon a weak plank in a great river. There he sits, and there he fears because he knows not certainly how long he shall sit there.

4. Doubtings, which are the suspensions or inhibitions (the holdings up) of the soul from any determinate inclinations one way or other, are the pausings of the mind.

For example, take a man on a journey. Where he meets with two ways, he looks on this and inclines it may be the right, and then he looks on that and supposes it may be the right, and then he looks upon both and makes a stand, and goes on in neither. So it is with the soul in doubtings (spiritually). There are two ways before it; two objects, two works, to believe or not to believe, and arguments to incline to the one and to the other, drawing into some equality of strength and weight; just like a pair of scales, answerably balanced, so that both are at a stand. There is no turning either to the right hand nor to the left. Therefore the schoolmen say well, that doubt is a mulling over each element of a contradiction, with fear of settling either part of it. That you may yet conceive this clearly, remember:

1) In our minds there are assentings, which are the adherents of the understanding to truths known. And there are dessentings, which are the bearings off from those truths. There the soul positively inclines; here it declines; there it puts out the hand, and here it keeps it in.

2) Doubtings properly stand between them

both. They are not plainly the one, or plainly the other. If I may speak freely, I conceive them to have a twang of either; they are *medium*, a middle thing, as your mixed colors are which you cannot style directly white or directly black.

The soul has a desire to join unto truth. It has a desire to share in that goodness which it apprehends; yet it neither fastens nor rejects, but, like the fish to the bait, it likes it and is striking at it, but dares not, and swims about. Or, like a wave of the sea (that is the Apostle's comparison, James 1:6), thrusting to the shore and yet drawing back; or, like a meteor hovering in the air, twists up and down. Such rolling, reeling actions of the soul are doubtings; they are a recoiling adventuring. The soul sees reason of either side, to draw and withdraw, to fire on and to fire back. It sees Christ and the promises, knows the goodness and bounty in the one and the other, whereupon it is giving on upon them, and putting out the hand, but then instantly it checks itself and is stayed with contrary arguments and fears. I may not be so bold; perhaps they belong not unto me so that the person is hanging between hope and fear. I would, but I may not. I may, but I dare not.

It is just with the soul as with those at chess. They set out a man and think to take a king, but then presently they are checked and draw him back again. God is my Lord and my King; nay and yet He is not. He will do me good, yet I fear He has not. He hears my prayer, yet I doubt He does not. My estate is good and happy, nevertheless I suspect it is not.

Thus a man wavers and rolls and is like a man in the ungrounded places. He no sooner plucks up one leg out of the dirt, but the other sinks in. The soul is not determined one way or the other.

3) One thing more, that though the mind does not pitch or rise unto a determinate action in spiritual doubtings, yet it ever inclines towards a determinate object: That is, though the doubting Christian cannot come yet to quit those uncertain, trembling, and shivering motions, and bring them to steadiness and positive fixing, yet his mind hones. It looks after Christ and the promises; it does not reject, nor does it give up all hopes. It keeps in it two things, which infidelity and despair lack:

a) One is that it prizes Christ and the promises, though it cannot clasp them.

b) Another is that it gives not up the case as desperate and impossible; but, though it cannot fix, yet it will be hovering about them.

Chapter 2

THE KINDS AND DIVERSITIES OF THEM

The second thing respects the sorts of doubtings, and these I must also touch.

I conjecture that there are four sorts of doubtings:

1. Some are of admiration. In these, the mind does not gainsay simply; no, it believes, and is only solicitous about the hidden manner or way of performance or accomplishment. Such a doubting was that of the Virgin, Luke 1:34. *How shall this be, seeing I know not a man?* "She does not doubt that it is to happen, but asks how it can happen," said St. Ambrose.

2. Others are of confirmation. This is where the soul believes, but desires something more to secure and settle it so that it might be put out of all doubt, as was that of Gideon's, Judges 6:36, 37, 39. These kinds of doubtings are the cravings of a little more indulgent security from God in matters of extraordinary concernment; not that we properly question the verity of Him, but that, in respect of ourselves, we might work the more confidently upon clearer evidence and warrant.

3. A third sort are of negation, and this is such a form of scrupling, wherein we plainly suspect God of His good work of truth, and is incident unto evil men in their general course, and to good men in respect of some particular carriages and businesses, as is evident in Zacharias, Luke 1:18. *Whereby shall I know this?* This question was a question of doubting, and this doubt-

ing, no question, was an unbelieving one. It did not credit the angel's message; so is it expressed, verse 20. *Thou shalt be dumb... because thou believest not My words.*

4. A fourth sort of inquietude, where the mind is diversly carried and is not come to a rest, as when a cause is not come to a sentence, but hangs in suspense. Now of this sort of doubtings we speak at this time, which again may be branched:

1) Into real, which questions the principles themselves, either for truth or goodness (and so they respect matters of faith), or else they question action touching lawfulness or unlawfulness (and so they respect matters of fact); in which respect they are more specially styled scruples of conscience, which are nothing else but some grating and painful doubts about points practical. Of these, see the Casuists.

2) Into personal, where not the things in themselves, but in respect of ourselves, are questioned and only questioned, not peremptorily denied or rejected, viz. I know and believe that God is a Father and Christ is a Redeemer and the Savior of sinners. I now doubt not whether there is any truth or good in these (for these I yield); but, upon view of my great sinfulness and many defects, I now only question (and this is enough) whether my interest is in that truth and goodness. What is said here of a case respecting spirituals, the same may be said of that other respecting the promises for temporals, because doubtings extend to both.

Again, there are two sorts of personal doubtings:

a) Some are privative, which remove all presence of faith. See 1 Timothy 2:8 and James 1:6.

b) Some are contrary, which *minuere,* but not

negare; they impair and keep faith low, but not wholly deny or extinguish it, as in our present text.

Chapter 3

OF THEIR POSSIBLE CONSISTENCE WITH FAITH

And here lies the kernel, whether personal doubtings, i.e. doubtings of a man's particular interest in God and Christ and the promises, may consist with personal faith.

To which I answer, they may; for (and mark it well), though:

1. Doubtings are sinful, they are the smokings of corruption.

2. They are no part of faith.

3. They cannot consist at the same instant with the acts of faith, for it is impossible that faith should formally doubt. As it is impossible that I should lay hand on the rock and not lay hand at the same time; or that mine eye should see and not see the color at the same time, or my hand receive and not receive the gift at the same time, so it is impossible that the soul, when it believes, should doubt. Forasmuch as faith in act and doubt in act are opposite, and the soul cannot possibly set out from one faculty at the same time opposite acts; I confess successively it may, yet simultaneously it cannot; but now, to believe and to doubt are opposite, for in the one I embrace, in the other I do not embrace; in the one I rest, in the other not etc.

4. Yet fourthly, actual doubting may be in a person who has habitual faith; for this you must know, that faith and doubtings are not opposed as life and death, where the presence of the one determinately con-

cludes the total absence of the other; but as cold and heat, in remiss degrees in the subject, where though the nature of cold is not the nature of heat, but naturally one is expulsive of the other, yet both lodge in the same room; so faith is not doubting, and doubting is not faith. One of these is expulsive of the other, yet both may, and do, meet in the same person who is, notwithstanding, called a believer from the most eminent part; for, as we truly call many persons beautiful, though in some one or other limb there may be some faulty incongruity in nature (because that which is better still denominates or gives the name), so we say that Christians are true believers because they have faith really in their souls, nowithstanding many culpable doubtings which they feel and express.

It would be folly indeed that men should think their fields had no corn because there are many filthy weeds, or that the heap has no wheat because there is much chaff; the pile no gold because there is much dross, or the soul no faith because there are many doubtings.

I had almost said (let it go, I think it is a truth) there is none had faith, but has found his doubtings. Did you ever see a fire without smoke? Smoke is no part of the fire, yet it steams from that fuel to which fire is put; so it is with faith and doubtings, etc.

Nay see this truth put out of all doubt by several instances in Scripture. Let this verse in Matthew 14:31 be the first, *O Thou of little faith* (said Christ to Peter), *Wherefore didst thou doubt?* where, though Christ reprehended him for doubting, yet, as He intimates his doubting, so his faith too. He had faith, though little, and doubtings, though he had that faith. There was the one, and there was the other. They were both in Peter; for he had not stepped out but for faith, and he had not sunk but for his doubtings.

Observe Abraham himself, *the father of the faithful;* yet we find him winding and turning, shuffling and doubting, more than once, if we read Genesis 12 and Genesis 15:2, 3, and Genesis 20.

So David had his trembling, his fainting, his suspicions; all in him was not faith. He, in his haste, falls out with some for liars, who yet spake nothing but the truth of God; and so again in his haste, he is *cut off from before the eyes of God,* who yet *heard the voice of his supplication.*

Job, also, *a man of great sorrows* and of great faith, yet had he not his qualms, his shakings, his questionings? Indeed, in some places, he seems heroic in his faith, graciously victorious over all calamities, and riding above all waves; yet in other places we find the man as well as the believer. He staggers; he fears; he is giving up.

The faithful in Scripture are compared oftentimes to trees which, though they are well-rooted, yet may be shaken; and to Noah's ark which, though it was a safe harbor, yet it was tossed; and to a house built on a rock which, though it is firm, and cannot be removed, yet it may be moved; and to stars which, though they are heavenly, yet are twinkling; and among them, much to the moon which, with her light has yet some dark spots.

What, should I allege examples? Let your own experiences and daily complaints sufficiently answer to this. Let them give verdict; some of you have not yet risen above your fears. Let God hold up His favor; do you not presently doubt? Let Him hold in His hand, do you not also doubt? O how we toss and roll and stagger in every sensible difficulty! In matters of this life, scarce a contrary occurrence which does not distract us. Thus is it with most of us in our infancy and in our settings out. But for you, who are of further perfection, who are ripened unto an assurance, perhaps unto a full assurance, can you never remember any bowings, shakings, shiverings, doubtings? Or think you never to meet with any more? I have known the sun one day bright, and the next covered; and David's mountain strong; but *Thou didst hide Thy face, and anon I was troubled,* Psalm 30.

Besides all this, consider the nature and condition of true faith in this life. It must then be granted that there may be doubtings with it, forasmuch as no grace is perfect in this life, it has its contrary in the same subject in some remiss degrees. And it is one work of faith still to be casting out of doubts which do rise in the mind, which working could not be unless there they were.

But you will say, "Whence should these arise? Does God alter in His life, in His nature, in His fidelity; or do the promises (which are the great stay of faith) up and come, ebb and flow? Do they vary from themselves, either for truth or goodness? Or is not Christ, the Foundation, the Rock on which our faith is built, is not He the *same yesterday, today, and forever?* If so, how, why, whence is it that a believer should doubt?"

I answer that, though there is the sameness in God, in Christ, in the Word, yet there is not a oneness in us; and the variations in us in no wise conclude anything in them, any more than the several alterations in the air infer a diversity in the sun, which is one and the same, in respect of itself. However, the changes are multiplied here below. Wherefore, know that the...

Chapter 4

SPRINGS, CAUSES, AND OCCASIONS OF DOUBTING ARE, OR MAY BE, THESE:

1. Natural corruption. This is a corrupt root, the seed of all sin and unbelief. This is that flesh which *lusts against the spirit* and thrusts up an abundance of motions, corrupt reasonings, and motives to interrupt our faith in its great business of believing. So that, when we would do good, evil is present with us and, when we would believe, unbelief is present with us.

It is very true that, in our conversion, the soul is graciously enlarged, and the powers of sin are crushed, yet still we go with a chain about our leg. And, though sin has its death-wound, yet so much life is still remaining as to interrupt out graces, to resist them; yea (and if we look not well unto it), to stay and bind them.

He who has a maim in his leg cannot move in that manner or measure as he desires; and a wounded hand or arm cannot stretch out itself and lay hold at all times. Corruption is in the best and will do its part, and that is one reason why we cannot do all our part in believing. You know, in the wars, how the intentions and motions of one side are stopped, and kept up by the malice of subtilty and power of the other; and that there may be many veins of sweetest water under the earth which yet are, many times, checked and controlled by the falling down of earth. O this body of sin, which (*nolentes volentes*) we must yet carry about with us! How backward is it to come to Christ? How unbelieving is it? How suspicious? How fearful? It will not be persuaded; it will not hearken; it will not credit; it will not yield; it will not embrace.

The very disciples who had the presence of Christ, who saw the miracles of Christ, who heard the voice of Christ, how often did they doubt, did they question? *Where shall we have bread to feed so many? We had trusted it should have been He who should have redeemed Israel;* so that Christ reproves them more than once or twice, *O slow of heart to believe,* &c. *Why do thoughts arise in your hearts? Behold My hands and My feet,* that it is I Myself. But Christ apologizes for them, *The spirit is willing, but the flesh is weak.*

2. Imperfection of faith. This is another cause of doubting. Why should a child fall so much, and a man so seldom? Is it not the weakness in the nerves, sinews, and low motive parts? When fire is newly kindled, it is but little, and has much smoke; so is it with our faith. The more imperfect it is, the more doubtings it finds.

Matthew 14:31. *O thou of little faith, wherefore didst thou doubt?* Little faith and great doubtings go together, like a little heat and great mists. Some men are but babes in Christ; they are but plants in the garden. They are but lambs in the fold. Now children are apt to fear, and plants to shake, and lambs to flag behind, and weak believers to doubt. Lay a little burden on a child's shoulder; he knows not what to do. Show him the water; he cries out. So is it with weak believers. Their strength is not proportioned unto unusual exigencies, neither have they experiences, nor that quickness of art to tie them to their helps; and these are great matters when a man lacks strength to deal with his enemy; and when he has not had experience. Therefore, let us consider this yet more that, where faith is weak or imperfect, there are three things incidental unto those believers:

1) They lack ability to argue, for their experience is little; and, therefore, their judgments are not so settled, so that they cannot always maintain their ground. David, because of former experiences, is not amazed at the uncircumcised Philistine, but rests upon that God for victory here who had granted him former deliverances from the bear and the lion. And so Paul confirms himself, 2 Corinthians 1:10, *who delivered us from so great a death, and does deliver, in whom we trust, that He will yet deliver;* but weak faith has little experience of God's truth, and of God's power, and of God's method and times.

2) They see their lacks and hindrances more than their helps and encouragements. They are like Elisha's servant, who saw the multitude of the enemies compassing the city with horses and chariots, and thereupon cried out, *Alas, my Master! How shall we do?* But, at first, he did not see the mountain full of horses and chariots of fire round about Elisha, which might have stayed and upheld him.

It is with new and weak believers as with the Israelites, who heard of the sons of Anak, those mighty giants, and of the high and mighty walls about the city of Canaan. They looked on these and were greatly perplexed and discouraged, but they did not look on the strong and Almighty God, who promised to go with them and conquer for them. So do these. They look upon the mere temptations and suggestions of Satan. They look upon the powerful stirrings of remaining corruption. They look upon the strength of present crosses; they look upon their own weaknesses against all these. They look upon God's delayings, upon their own dullness, and whatsoever may keep them down; but they do not look upon that God who has promised, who has performed the oath to Abraham, the father of the faithful. They do not look upon Christ, who has by His blood ratified and sealed the covenant. They do not look upon that mighty spirit of grace in them. They do not look upon other standing Christians, who can tell them that God is true in all His promises, and assuredly righteous and a present help, and who never fails them that trust upon Him and wait.

3) They cannot repair unto the establishments of faith as strong believers can. They are not yet so acquainted with the armory of faith, the promises. They are the armory of faith; but now these promises are many, and are graciously framed to the variety of our conditions which, because the beginning believer knows not, therefore in the times of changes, not being as ready, not having his weapons, is not as immediately able to send them out. Hence it is that doubtings do so arise; yea, and so grow upon him in such strength that he is likely to faint.

You shall experimentally find many good people who have, in some cases, maintained their ground with credit to their faith (for they have traversed a particular vein of the promises; they have found them out; they have applied them and made use of them by virtue of which they have borne down the many risings of doubt and fear in that kind, and have singularly enabled and comforted their hearts against distrust and fear). But these self-same persons all of a sudden have been, and are, strangely puzzled, distressed, afraid, doubtful, full of fears and dejections, and all that they can do is to bear up. Yea, and that is hardly done, too. Why? What is the matter? Have they no faith? Yes, and does not that faith work? Perhaps it does in a general way, but with particular efficacy they cannot yet observe it.

How so? This: there is a new kind of trouble, a new burden, which yet they were not put unto, and they cannot find any promise to reach that same. And hence it is that their fears and doubtings exceedingly sprout up and distract them. And this is found to be very true, that in particular and sensible distresses (be the matter and kind what they may be), the soul remains in hurried perplexity, in a wavering unsettledness, until that faith can find out a promise to answer it, either expressly or virtually. One of these ways it must reach us in our conditions, or else our fears are up.

3. The studying of the life of sense. This is another spring of doubting, which is evident in Thomas, John 20:25, *Except I shall see in His hands the print of the nails, and thrust my hand into His side, I will not believe.* He must see and feel, or else he is faithless.

Now to study the life of sense is this: to place the disposition of God, and the issues of our condition, in our feelings and sensible apprehensions so as to believe that God is my God because I find Him so; that He is gracious because I find a sensible answer of my prayers; that He accepts my services because I find that life of affections; so, on the contrary, that He is not my God because I do not find those sensible reports of His favor. I do not find that quickness and former smartness of affections; I do not find immediate answers to all my desires and requests; that I am not in the estate of grace because I do not feel the vigors and secret increasings of grace; that I do not believe because I do not rejoice or see my sins blotted out, etc; which kind of life must verily be exposed unto infinite and continual doubtings for:

1) The soul here has no constant bottom to settle upon. Our feeling is sometimes more, sometimes less, sometimes none at all. Indeed, it is true that faith may breed feeling, but then it is as true that faith may be without it. As the soul breeds seeing and hearing in the eyes and ears, yet the soul may be in the man when these do not see and these do not hear. A man cannot but be perplexed in his thoughts if he holds this opinion, that meat does not nourish him unless he immediately sees how the parts grow bigger by it; or that his father does not love him because he is not always smoothing and stroking him; or that his seed is lost because it is not a present harvest; or that the channel will shortly be dry and without water because the tide is gone out and has left it naked. In like manner, to conclude against our souls from sensibles and mutables exposes it to the labyrinth of daily fears and scruples.

2) But, secondly, the soul hereby advantages Satan in his suggestions; for the life of sense (like the rolling sea) is open to all winds. It has a secret, restless, unquiet distemper of its own; but besides that, it is open to the singular disturbances and inquietude from the devil, for the life of sense has made two propositions for him of the despairing syllogism, and he can easily make the other, viz. he who does not have the sense of God's favor, present answers from God, feel-

ings of His graces in their nature and measure, cannot be in the state of grace and salvation (This is the maxim of sense); "but you," says Satan, "do not have the sense of God's favor, etc." "Ergo," says he, "you are not."

"Ergo also," say you, "I am not in the state of grace and salvation."

Lo, here the issues of the life of sense! And now, no marvel if the soul does not live upon Christ or the promises, but is tossed to and fro, and hangs in extreme suspense.

3) Yet, thirdly, it is a life which much dishonors God and, therefore, is exposed to many fears and unsettledness. What, to measure the truths of God by our sense? What is this but to arraign God both for truth and graciousness? What is this but to set upon God and give the sentence, which He has kept in His own hands? What is this, but to limit the holy One of Israel; yea, to correct His wisdom as not being skillful to order the business of our salvation, unless we always have an eye or a finger at every turn to know His particular intentions and proceedings with us? It is a glorious and singular way to believe so long, until we come down to feeling; but to begin with feeling, and so rise to believing, is a delusion both dangerous and impossible; for you can never truly feel, unless you first believe. Can you truly warm your heart with that divine favor which faith did not let in?

4. A fourth cause of doubtings is when we deny faith its matter and grounds to work. How is that? It is when we guide the whole business below and not above. I will give you some instances:

1) You know that the condition of grace is

exposed to many short allowances in externals; and the condition of sinful men is capable of large prosperity in worldly things. A good man may have many wants, and an evil man may have, in this life, his good things (as Abraham speaks of Dives). Now, when a person looks upon the bulk, upon the outward part, upon the shell, upon the rind of things, and sees plenty with evil men, and poverty with good men; honor shining there, and contempt clouding here; fullness for them, and leanness for these; pleasures and liberties attending them, and sorrows and restraints befalling these; when, I say, he looks on this, and no higher than this, it is possible that suspicions and doubtings may start up. It is possible that the soul may sink down somewhat at it. See an evidence in Asaph, Psalm 73:2. *My feet were almost gone; my steps had well-nigh slipped. 3. When I saw the prosperity of the wicked. 12. These are the ungodly who prosper in the world; they increase in riches. 13. Verily I have cleansed my heart in vain, and washed my hands in innocency. 14. For all the day long have I been plagued, and chastened every morning.* Observe here his distrusts and doubts, as if his gracious course in no way benefited him, or as if he had served God for naught. And thus he goes on, while he bends his thoughts downward, whil he keeps in his faith, while he denies it matter to work upon; but (verse 17), there he gives scope for faith to work, and then he is free again, and well again. [*Until I went into the sanctuary of God, then I understood their end.*]

2) In case of the sinful condition. While we look on it, and deny faith its matter also to work upon, we shall be full of doubtings. Let a man look only upon his sins, upon the nature of them, the aggravations of

them, what will come of it?

a) Strong humiliations, and those are good.

b) Doubtings and despairs, and those are bad. The single considerations of sin are the matter only of our fear; they are a grievous burden. David was not able to stand under it, *My sins are too heavy a burden for me to bear,* Psalm 38:4.

For what hope is there in ourselves? What is in a sinner to uphold a sinner? No burden is an ease to itself. Let people behold their sins, and not use their faith. They cannot but doubt, for now sin appears in all the motives and causes of fear, and now God appears not in the nature of a friend, but with the countenance of an enemy and of a severe judge. And where now can the troubled soul anchor, or fasten, or ease itself?

God, you know, has given unto man two ears and two eyes. If we make use of one only, our lives will often hang in doubt and suspense. If we do not have an ear to hear what God says to a humbled sinner, as well as an ear to hear what conscience will say unto a sinner; if we do not have an eye to look unto Christ, as well as an eye to look unto our sins; an eye to behold the biting fiery serpent, we cannot then but doubt. We must give faith its scope to work upon Christ, else we shall neither be freed from our doubtings, nor yet from our sins which cause those doubtings.

3) In case of bodily distractions and occurrences which put us into an exigence or strait if we look below only, if we look upon their strength and our strength only, it will now be with us as with David, tired out, and almost spent by the huntings and pursuings of Saul, *I shall surely one day fall by the hand of Saul;* or as with Peter, who, looking upon the waves and not upon

Christ, began to sink and cried, *Lord, save me;* or as with Jehoshaphat, while he looked upon the great armies, *We know not what to do.*

Not long since, we might have read this in our very faces, when the churches abroad were in great distress. We looked on their dust and ashes, their ruins and weakness; we looked on man and gave all up for lost. We did not look upon God and, therefore, our ship was full of water. Our hearts failed us; doubts and fears, like a black cloud, overspread us. Nay, at this very time, we hear of an externally disproportionate strength that the enemies are more in number. They are confederate; they plot; they intend a great design, and now I find the fears, the doubts wagging and, assuredly, while we look downward only and not upward. While we lay events and issues upon the creature; while we give faith no scope to look up and work upon that God who can save by a few as well as by many, we shall never be freed from doubtings. The very same is true in our personal occurrences. As long as we look on the things only which we meet with, and oppose our own strength unto them, it will be with us as a house without pillars, tottering with every blast; or, as with a ship without an anchor, tossed with every wave, for every cross is too hard for us, though none can be too hard for God.

4) So, for temptations, here also our doubtings fly up because or faith does not fly out. O (say we) we are not able to bear, to withstand, to overcome! The temptations are strong, and many, and daily. Suppose so, and what do we? Verily, we are soon ready to sit down and to give the day to Satan, never considering that God gives His soldiers His arms; never considering

that the quarrel and battle is the Lord's. He is engaged in the fight, for all is for His sake. We think that God only looks on, and believe not how much He curbs Satan and sustains us; as if Satan might do what he pleased, and God left us alone to grapple; whereas, the Lord makes manifest His power in our weakness, and His grace is sufficient for us, and He will bruise Satan shortly under our feet.

5. A fifth cause of doubtings may be particular and special sins after conversion, which are, like water, dropped into a candle, making it to burn flat and dull, with a black snuff at the top, and catching, as it were, going up and down for hold; or, as a discharge, a salty discharge, fallen into the eyes, which intercepts the sight and darkens it for a time. So do our special sins after conversion. They dim and darken the soul; and, like those enclosed spirits of the air, in the bowels of the earth, they cause many fearful shakings and tremblings, as is evident in David after his great sins of adultery and murder. They exceedingly weakened his spiritual condition and wiped off all his comforts.

Beloved, these sins must be a strong spring of doubtings if we do but consider:

1) That it is their nature to set us off from the shore and harbor. You know that a ship which lies quiet in the harbor, or by the shore, thrust it out, launch it into the sea, it is tossed again. Now, in all known sins which wound the conscience (after conversion), we loose the anchor and put off: The promises and Christ (upon which our confidences were anchored), they now seem to give; they will leave; they will withdraw.

But suppose, in their sensible virtue, they should

not (which yet they do). Nevertheless, we cannot fasten now, for the very temper of the soul is injured. Our spirit is wounded. You know, though the staff stands where it did, and as it did, yet if my hand is wounded, I cannot clasp it, nor use it as formerly.

Now, what do you think? Must not the soul be filled with fears and with doubts, which has thrust itself thus from such a gracious harbor as the mercies, the loving kindnesses, the sweet and blessed promises of God? May it not say now, as David said once, Psalm 77:3, *I remembered God, and was troubled;* and well may you be troubled who would, for such a sin, pull away your hand from such a God.

2) God really takes these sins ill, very ill, from those upon whom He has conferred such fruits of His love. For this is a truth, that in case of offenses, love and bounty can give in the strongest and heaviest aggravations, as in that of David, 2 Samuel 12:7, *I anointed thee king over Israel, and I delivered thee out of the hand of Saul. 8. And I gave thee thy master's house, and gave thee the house of Israel and Judah; and if that had been too little, I would, moreover, have given unto thee such and such things. 9. Wherefore hast thou despised the commandment of the Lord to do evil in His sight, &c. ?*

Observe how the Lord pleads and aggravates it upon David. Now, when a child knows that he has committed a fault (concerning which his father gave him a special charge, see you do it not), and withal he knows that his father is fully acquainted with all the business; it is likely (we find it so) that fears and doubtings gather within the breast of the child; he dares not keep off, and yet he is afraid to come in. He knows that his father has taken it ill at his hands. So it is with us after our special sins. We know that God hates them. He hates them not personally, but naturally; not because in such persons, but because in any persons their nature is repugnant to His. As we hate poison for itself, and, therefore, let it be in a toad or in a prince's cabin, we hate it still; and they now have fallen upon such sins, and have incensed a gracious Father. What notable fears, what strange misgivings, what appallings get up now upon the heart?

"Where is my father," said the offending child? He is within (says one); away he runs, or he is abroad, and then down he sits, and weeps, and bewails his loss. I shall never gain his favor again.

Thus it is with us after our special sins. If God seems to draw towards us, we are ready to fly from Him. *I heard Thy voice,* (said Adam), *and was afraid, and hid myself.* And, if He does not draw towards us, we sit down, wring our souls, and fetch many a deep "Ah, Ah! What have I done! Ah me, what, where am I now? I have provoked my God, and am afraid to come unto Him."

3) God does not easily open His favor unto those who thus abuse it. There was free intercourse between God and the soul before, but now the door is shut which before was open, and God Himself will keep the key, so that nothing, no means or ways, shall open unto us, until He pleases. You remember how David kept his distance from Absalom for his lewdness; he kept him off a long time so that he might not see the king's face. And David himself, for his sins against his father, could not, without long suings, see the face of God, as before, Psalm 51.

And now, do you think it strange that the soul

should doubt? Assuredly, great desires delayed and prolonged, cause great fears. Yea, it breeds singular suspicions; maybe I shall be still put off. *Will the Lord cast off for ever? And will He be favorable no more?* Psalm 77:7.

4) No, now the soul, being made sensible and having weighed all circumstances, can, and does, teach itself many arguments and reasons to keep off. It is apt enough to fall upon itself and to keep down any readiness which it observes to give on upon God or Christ.

It is some time before faith can find a way to ingratiate this offending soul and to find a sufficient medium through which it may close with God for pardon and favor. And when faith has found it out, then our misgiving hearts beat us off; and, as our weak children pluck down the bird soaring up with a string, so do our weak hearts pull in our faith, which is now speeding towards heaven by the blood of Jesus Christ for us.

The more tenderness we gain of the sins, the more shyness and fear grow on us; and seldom does the soul recover its former hold and ancient correspondence and intimateness with God, until there has been a proportional humiliation and spaces of settled reformation, between which, and the great discovery of special and renewed assurance, the heart meets with many a wave, with many a sad day, with many a fearful rinsing, with many strong and terrible doubtings.

So, then, you see that special sins after conversion cause great doubtings in the soul because they make a jar, a wound. They lay a bar between us and God. They keep up God and keep down faith, and give up all the matters of disheartening and fear. They make the soul to be at a stand, to go away from the gates of heaven, many times, with singular checks and heaviness.

6. A sixth cause of doubtings may be indispositions unto, or about, spiritual duties: when our altar seems to have no fire, our bodies to have no souls, our affections to be estranged from our services; when we pray, but not with that fervency; when we hear, but not with that attentiveness; when we set upon any sort of duty, but not with that alacrity, with that joy, with those becoming spirits.

Nay, sometimes there is a strange listlessness, a kind of flat dullness or drowsiness, so that we hardly move upon our work, much ado to draw ourselves unto duty. Like the disciples, the soul is so heavy that it can hardly watch and pray. Out of which kind of slumberings, the hearts of Christians ordinarily awake with doubtings, and that about two particulars especially:

1) One respects the verity and being of grace. As it was with Gideon, in another case, Judges 6:13, *If the Lord be with us, why then is all this befallen us?* So here, if truth of grace were in me, how should all these indispositions, dullnesses, deadnesses, accompany me? Where the spirit of Christ is, there is liberty, but I am as one chained up. Where grace is truly kindled, there is a holy fire to warm the heart in duty; *I have rejoiced in the way of Thy testimonies,* (Psalm 119:14) *and with my whole heart have I sought Thee,* So it was with David. *Thy word was unto me, the joy and rejoicing of my heart, for I am called by Thy name, O Lord of Hosts,* says Jeremiah 15:16. And the prophet Isaiah, in chapter 56:7 said, *God will make His people joyful in His house of prayer.* And, besides all this, we are commanded to *serve the Lord with gladness,* Psalm 100:2. Whereupon the soul misgives, how can my condition be good, which differs so much from

the secret and lively dispositions of grace? How can it
be good, which is so unanswerable to that quickness
promised and found in the people of God? How can I
be good who, about the actions of good, are so dull
and heavy, awkward and slow?

2) But, then, suppose the soul can clear and
absolve itself from this fear (by knowing that fire may
be where it does not always flame, and the root may
live where the branches do not always flourish, and by
finding some answerable dullnesses in some eminent
David's, who often have prayed for quickening). Yet
there arises another doubting from our dullness and
indisposition, which is a fear of acceptance. The Lord
will not accept these services because they are so heavy;
they are, therefore, without any efficacy. Suppose I may
be good, yet they are bad, and can win no favor with
God. Thus the soul is, often times, greatly perplexed by
reason of its indispositions; as if either it were totally
bad, or God intended little good unto it, because it is
not quickened and more enlivened in the services presented unto Him. And, verily, it will greatly trouble a
tender and sincere heart to observe in itself such flat
and dull opinions of God and Christ, and such an in-
aptitude in itself in doing that which, to do with the
best of its strength, and might, and affections, it sees
reasons and has desires thereto.

7. A seventh spring or occasion of doubtings may
be fruitless endeavors. I call them so because we think
them so. What is that? This it is, when we find our defects in our particular graces and in particular duties,
or some effects of particular corruptions, and have
gone to God by prayer and in His ordinances, so that
we have a long time prayed for the filling up and

enlarging of our weak faith, love, sorrow, joy, assurance; and prayed against that hardness, passion, or whatsoever sinfulness is observed in the heart. And yet we seem to be still where we were. We creep on with the same impotencies in grace and move on with the same burdens of sinful motions and propensions. O now the soul sits down with much sorrow and with doleful conclusions! "Well, it is in vain to seek any more. God will make that good to me, which He threatened unto Moab, Isaiah 16:12, *He shall come unto His sanctuary and shall not prevail.* I have sought Him a long time and have not prevailed. I shall never rise above these risings. If God had a purpose to do me good, I should have been spared ere this."

This opinion of "success-lessness" must cause doubtings because:

1) God seems to have a controversy with the soul. "Surely," says the heart, "something is the matter that I cannot have an audience. All is not right and even between God and me."

2) The very stays and supports of duty seem to fail us. You know that the promises are the great encouragements of all our services; and what have we to bind God but His own promises, by which He has bound Himself. He has said that He will hear and answer; upon which assurance of His we came in and prayed, but cannot get any thing, though we press God upon His own promise. Whereupon, the soul is brought to a stand, "If God will not answer His own work, how shall He answer me?"

3) Now we suspect not our own petitions, but our persons; and we uncomfortably judge or fear that we have been deceived in our progress towards heaven.

God would be to us as this (a God hearing prayers) if we had been to God as His, serving Him with a perfect heart, for *God heareth not sinners,* John 9:31. But, *If any man be a worshipper of God, and doth His will, him He heareth.* Whereupon the soul strongly argues against itself, "My heart is sinful, or else my prayers would have been successful. I regard iniquity in my heart; therefore it is that the Lord hears me not," Psalm 66:18. Beloved, you who heal with observation and experience can acknowledge:

a) That there are spaces between our prayers and God's answers. God hearkens what David speaks, and David must hearken what God will speak. Prayer is our angle, our seed, our dove, our messenger; it does not always take at first. It does not always return a present harvest; it comes in sooner, and sometimes later. It waits the time of the Master.

b) God is wise in causing these spaces. He has ends, singular ends, both for His own glory, and for the good of our graces.

c) But, thirdly, corruption takes occasion hereby, and Satan vents his envious malice hereupon, as the backbiters, slanderers, and contentious spirits, who love to set variance. Between faithful friends, let the least occasion happen, a wry look, a misplaced word, a misintended neglect, a forbearing of present dispatch in some desired service. Let these fall out, immediately the backbiter, envious, malicious, contentious spirit catches. Lo, you see his life, his backwardness, his slighting of you, etc.

This is what our corrupt hearts and Satan do. Look, you see how needless, how fruitless all the care and service of God is. Alas, He does not think on you; He does not regard your prayers. If He had loved you, if He intended to do you good, how could this be? Would He have held up after so many prayers so many tears, so many importunities, so many pressings, by His mercies, by His Christ, by His promises? No, no, you are not in favor with God. His mercies, His promises do not belong to you.

8. An eighth spring may be imbecility of judgment about the essentials of salvation; and, assuredly, here lies the great spring of doubtings. An erroneous mind is the forge which hammers all our suspicions; it is the womb which bears and breeds all our fears; if it does not find, yet it makes all our knots for us.

One man spoke of a plain place of Scripture. "This verse," said he, "would have been easy, had not commentators made it so knotty." That is what we say of a Christian's condition. It is gracious, happy, clear, sure, if erroneous judgments did not disturb, vex, and unsettle them. This is true, that a weak judgment and a tender conscience are seldom without fear and doubting. You see it in the Romans, about practical matters, whereupon the apostle presses the stronger *not to receive the weak to doubtful disputations;* and, if they had a particular faith, to keep it unto themselves, knowing well how weak judgments, like weak plants, are easily stirred and shaken.

You may see it also in the Ephesians about doctrinal matters; for Paul, giving an item unto them to *overthrow their childishness,* (Ephesians 4:14) he paraphrases it to be such an estate, wherein men are tossed to and fro, and carried about with every wind.

Two things are incident unto shallow judgments, by virtue of which they are objected, with ease, unto doubtings:

1) One is, they have not been conversant in the compass of truths; there are some truths which they know not. They have not all their holds and strength.

2) New doctrines, contrary to old truths, are not so easily over-mastered by their understandings, but either win misbelief, or else disturb true belief. You shall scarcely hear any new things started but, withal, we hear of many persons startled, as if their faith had hitherto been in vain; for tender consciences are apt to believe the most and, therefore, sometimes believe those points which are false.

Shall I give you instances among ourselves?

One is an equality of humiliation before conversion; as if no man were truly converted, who has not equaled the greatest penitent in the highest degrees of contrition and terror. And hence it is that many distressed, bowed, broken souls exceedingly labor to grind themselves and to fall into the flames of horrible fear, thereby to assure themselves of a good estate. Whereas, all Christians are not equal in their preparations; and no man can judge his estate simply by legal humiliation.

Another is a full assurance at first, or else no faith. It is as if Jacob's ladder had no degrees, and the sun, at his first peeping, was in the height of heaven; or, that a scholar must be placed in the upper form as soon as he enters the school. Such inconsiderate deliveries as these trouble the faith of many, as the apostle speaks of those in 2 Timothy 2:18.

"If faith cannot be without full assurance, then I am no believer," said David, "for I had my faintings."

"Nor I," said Peter, "for Christ Himself tells you I

had my doubtings."

It is a most vain and dangerous way for any divine or ordinary Christian to impose rules and to deliver a thing as a dogmatically and common truth which they have, in a special way, only observed in themselves. The Spirit of God bestows upon all the elect of God the same substantial frame of grace, but the making up, and the making out of these is different. As no man must say he has no soul because he does not feel those particular workings of reason and desire which another does; so no man must conclude another to be out of the estate of grace if haply there is not a plenary answerableness in them both for every method and measure of working grace.

Therefore, let me caveat a little here to you who are grown Christians. Remember that there are some who are weak, yet true members of the same body; and do you not indiscreetly insist upon your only personal experiences (and those only in some particulars) in all companies because you have, perhaps, risen high; therefore, none are right who are below you. Consult the Scriptures and deliver to us what it directs and wherein it supports. You do not yet know the aptness in tender consciences to throw down themselves and to catch at matters and arguments of trouble. You send, perhaps, from your company a poor, a laden, and troubled heart with a bitter and amazed opinion that it has no faith, which yet came unto you with some weak and strong desires of firmer faith.

Weak judgments, as I said before, cannot bear all things; but, like some men's stomachs, are immediately oppressed with unusual meats. And, when we have mistaken an error for truth, it may prove to the soul as the mistaking of poison for medicine, a business of troublesome and dangerous consequence.

9. Ignorance of the doctrine of justification is another cause of doubting.

The doctrine of justification is a doctrine of life, Romans 5:18, *The free gift came upon all men unto justification of life.* And it is a doctrine of peace, Romans 5:1, *Being justified by faith, we have peace with God.* And, therefore, the ignorance of it must be a cause of fear and doubting.

Here, consider four things:

1) The Christian condition is subject to many sensible impressions. We are seldom without assault or combat, and those pierce us most which the conscience throws up. A man may bear any wound with more ease than that which he has given himself. When the law powerfully reveals, and the conscience closely applies the guilt of our nature and lives, now it is a sad and heavy time. Job cries out in the sense of this sting, chapter 13:26, *Thou writest bitter things against me, and makest me to possess the iniquities of my youth.* Solomon tells us that the wounded spirit is hardly sustained, Proverbs 18:14. David is even dried up by his roaring and worn away with the pain of it; and Paul cries out as a man almost lost, Romans 7.

2) The soul makes out at such a time for some stay and help. It seeks where it may lay his burden and find something to ease and deliver. It is with a sick soul as with a sick body, which turns from one side to another, from this part to the other part of the bed, and of the pillow, and craves help of this friend and of another. It would have ease from any, but perchance can get none from all.

"Here is sin," says the person. "Here is a sinful soul, and there is a righteous law broken, and a righteous God offended who yet must and will be satisfied. He calls upon me, and has arrested my conscience. Now, good Lord, what shall I do? I have nothing to pay, or that can give satisfaction." *Wherewith shall I come before the Lord, and bow myself before the high God? Shall I come before him with burnt offerings, with calves of a year old? Will the Lord be pleased with thousands of rams, or with ten thousands of rivers of oil? Shall I give my firstborn for my transgression, the fruit of my body for the sin of my soul?* Micah 6:6. Those are nothing; those can do nothing; my sins are many, great, and deep. My righteousness is none, or too weak to answer for my unrighteousness; all the good I have, or can do, cannot expiate the evil which I have done or make up that good which I should have. Here is some sorrow, but what is that? It is but as a drop to the ocean of guilt which lies upon me. Here is some duty, but what is that? It is defective in itself, and no amends to the many thousands of breaches which I have made.

3) The soul cannot stay itself upon itself. God calls for satisfaction. "I do not have it," says the soul. "God will have satisfaction. Lord! What shall I now do?" The conscience works upon us and tells us God is just; and, if these sins are not pardoned, and a righteousness found and presented, we are lost. Now, the soul is at a stand seriously and sadly thinks, "What do I have? Nothing but sin; yet sin cannot answer for sin. Perhaps some imperfect holiness, but that cannot make a perfect satisfaction."

O my brethren! Our blood and spirits must go and come when the arrest is upon us, and none appears to bail us; when the ship is split, and no rock is near to save us; when the sentence of death is read against us, and none is at hand to pardon us; when the avenger of blood pursues us, and no city of refuge opens to shelter us: unrighteousness, inability, and conscience, and God meet; and none yet. Nothing is yet found to answer for us or to pacify Him.

4) Without us, there is something able to stay us, of which the soul, being ignorant, is still perplexed. It cannot conclude its fears, and scruples, and doubts.

What is that? I answer, Justification is the stay and, therefore, the soul must be burdened, being unacquainted with it.

For example:

a) Till we know where to lay down our sinful burden, we must be troubled. If a perplexed soul could find any to charge his debts upon, who would bear and answer for him, then it might have rest. Now, Christ, in justification, takes our guilt upon Him. As Paul said to Philemon, concerning his servant, Onesimus, *If he has wronged thee, or oweth thee ought, put that upon mine account,* so said Christ to the broken and laden sinner, "If you have any guilt and sinful debts to be answered for to God, put them upon My account. If you have wronged My Father, I will make all even. Look for your discharge and acquittance by Me, for I was made sin for you that you might be made the righteousness of God in Me," 2 Corinthians 5:21. "And God was in Me, (verse 19) *reconciling the world unto Himself, not imputing their trespasses unto them.*" And, 1 John 2:1, *If any man sin, he hath an advocate with the Father, etc.*

b) Till we know our justifying righteousness, we cannot but be troubled. No righteousness justifies but that which is in every way perfect and full. Now, this is in Christ and not in us. Romans 5:19, *By the obedience of one, many shall be made righteous.* When a sinner is to stand before God for acceptance and life, he does not stand before Him in his own rags, but in the garment of his eldest Brother. He cannot say, "Lord, here is a righteousness in me which has fulfilled Thy law; here is a righteousness in me against which Thou can make no exception; here is a righteousness in me for which Thou are to account and pronounce me just." But this he may say: "Lord, though I have no perfect righteousness to answer Thee, yet Thy Son has for me, and He is made unto me from Thyself, my *righteousness, wisdom, sanctification, and redemption,*" 1 Corinthians 1:30. And, *being justified by faith* in it, he may *have peace with God, through our Lord Jesus Christ,* Romans 5:1.

Brethren, no man can be free from strong fears and doubts who thinks to be acquitted or condemned by what is in himself. If a man thinks this: "The Lord will, or does, enter into judgment with me, and I find nothing to satisfy Him. All the powers of my heart and of my graces are insufficient; and, therefore, there is now no hope but that I shall be cast and condemned." You see, here is ground of doubtings; yet, if a man could look out of himself and know that his righteousness is to be found in Christ and God has appointed it so, that I am to be justified by that righteousness only, now, the soul may have a stay to rest on. Yet my Savior's righteousness was perfect, was accepted; and He is mine, and His righteousness mine.

c) Till we know the dispositions (if I may so speak) in God about our justifying, we cannot but doubt. For a man reasons thus: "I have committed great sins which now grieve me; and I hate them, and I have left them, but I do not know how they may be pardoned." Those will now cause doubtings until we know that God, for Christ, will justify us from great sins as well as small, 1 Corinthians 6:9-10, and that He blots out the thick cloud as well as the cloud, Isaiah 44:22. *I have blotted out, as a thick cloud, thy transgressions; and as a cloud, thy sins.* And that there were expiatory sacrifices not only for infirmities, but also for enormities, all which typified the virtue of the blood of Christ, which justifies from great sins.

But I have nothing to move God to pardon them. Yet, pardoning is a gracious work. God pardons sins, not for your sake, but for His own sake, Isaiah 43:25. *I, even I, am He that blotteth out thy transgressions for My own sake,* and for His Christ's sake, Ephesians 1:7. *In whom only have we redemption, even the forgiveness of our sins.*

"But God will call me hereafter to account again, though, for a while, He seems to be graciously pleased." No, the Lord in His new covenant of grace assures the contrary. Jeremiah 31:34, *I will forgive their iniquity, and I will remember their sin no more.* So that you manifestly see how the ignorance of our justification leaves the soul in great doubtings, because: a man knows not where to cast his burden; where to find his righteousness.; what is the virtue, fullness, love, and graciousness, the fidelity and irrevocableness of God in justifying a sinner by Christ?

10. A tenth cause of doubtings is disputation against the promises. You have heard, heretofore, that the ignorance of the promises is an occasion of doubting; and now I am to show you that the arguing of the soul against them is also another cause.

But you will say, "Does any man dare to dispute against God's promises?" I answer, the promises may be considered:

1) In respect of their absolute truth and goodness. Thus, they are not disputed against unless by atheists and positive unbelievers, as were those scoffers, 2 Peter 3:4, who said, *Where is the promise of His coming?*

2) In respect of their application and extent. Thus, many weak believers are subject to argue against them; not whether they are verity and mercy; not whether righteousness and peace meet in them; but whether these reach to them, and may be applied by them. Nay, that is not all. They oftentimes, upon unjust grounds, thrust away the promises from themselves. And now the soul must be hurried with fears and doubtings, in case the condition is sensible because:

a) The promises are to faith as ground unto the anchor. Cast out an anchor and, if it has no ground to fasten or hitch in, the ship rolls still. This is a truth: if faith cannot pitch and fix, the soul cannot be quiet and settled. David, in one place, uses the comparison of a bird, that his soul flew unto God as a bird unto her nest. While the bird is in the air, it is hovering, flying, and restless; so is it with the soul, until faith can settle it under the wings of a promise.

Nay, again, the promises are called *the breasts of consolation.* When the child is hungry and distempered, nothing quiets it but the breast; and, assuredly, if the promises do not still the soul, nothing can. Now, when a man will move from this ground of faith, when he will fly from his rest, when he refuses the breasts of consolation, no marvel if his soul is full of doubts and fears; for this is all one. It is as if a lame man should throw away his crutches, or a weak man his staff, or a sick man his cordials, or a sinking man the bow which holds him up. The goodness of the Lord promised to David was that which held up all his fainting; and so all God's people have still been held and staffed up by God's work; and, therefore, that person must be full of doubts who withdraws his shoulder from such a stay and rock upon which he should lean and rest himself.

b) This is but selfishness, which is ever accompanied with unquietness; for why do you refuse to apply those promises which God has made? Is it not because: you would have more goodness first; and less unbelief first? And is not this a self-seeking, yea, in some sort, a self-standing? What an odd and unseemly method of worshipping God is this: "Lord, I have but weak grace, and Thou hast promised to strengthen it, perfect, and finish it; but I will not believe Thy promise belongs to me until I have first a greater increase of my grace."

Or thus, "Lord, I find much unevenness in duty, and Thou hast promised to give Thy Spirit, which shall cause me to walk in Thy way; but I will not believe this promise until I am first more enabled in duty."

Or thus, "Lord, I find much sinfulness in me, and Thou hast promised to change and cleanse the heart and to subdue iniquity; but I will not believe this promise until first I see my sins subdued. When I find my graces increased, then I will believe Thou will increase them. When I find my obedience continued and my sins subdued, then will I believe that Thou will cause me to walk and will subdue my sins. If Thou will perform Thy promise before I believe Thy promise, then I will believe Thy promise." This is as if a man would see the blood in the veins before they are opened; or wash his hands clean before he has turned the faucet to let out the water.

c) A man is still held by the powers of his corruption; and, where corruptions or wants are still found in their former measure, there the tender soul will doubt and fear.

Let a man bestow himself much in hearing, or much in praying, or much in conferring; yet, if he has the art of thrusting away the promises, he will still be as he was. Suppose a man is sick and calls unto his help a college of physicians. Let them consult upon his state, prescribe the most fitting potions and quickening cordials and, when the patient has heard them, he refuses their prescriptions. He will not take them, but says, "These do not belong to me." Will his disease at all abate? So it is with us. When we hear, or read, or confer, and many promises fall in to our help; if we put them aside, we now keep up our sinfulness, our weaknesses, and, therefore, keep up our doubtings and distrusts.

"But," you will say, "all promises cannot be applied by all men, in all conditions, and therefore good reason for us to hold off." To which (briefly) I answer thus: Though all promises cannot be applied by all men at one time, yet some promises may be applied by a humbled and sensible sinner at some time or other.

Suppose you feel the power of sin stirring in its motions and workings and (as Paul complains) leading you captive. Though every promise cannot now be applied, yet you do ill in not fastening on the promises of mortification, which are made for this end: that the sensible and weary sinner should lay hold on them for the subduing of his sins.

Again, suppose you find weakness of grace that you cannot do the good that you would do. Do you now do well to thrust away the promises of assistance and strengthening by saying, "What is that to me, if God has said, 'I will uphold, and I will strengthen, and My grace is sufficient, and My power shall be manifest in weakness'"?

So again, suppose you feel the guilt of sin piercing and afflicting your conscience, and God has promised to pardon iniquities, transgressions, and sins, to love freely and to receive graciously. Do you now do well or wisely to thrust away the pardoning promises and say, "What are they to such a one as I am?" It is as if a beggar should say, "What is it to me that there are bountiful alms at the rich man's gate?" or a malefactor, "What is it to me that the prince will pardon traitors?" or a sensible sinner, "What is it to me that Christ died for sins, and God will be merciful to returning sinners?"

11. An eleventh cause of doubtings may be the suspension of divine favor. When God holds up His countenance, the light of it from shining into the heart, so that a Christian does not enjoy his day as before, his God as before, in the sensible evidences of His loving favor, now the soul may possibly fall into singular distrusts and fears. See it in David, Psalm 30:7. *Lord, by Thy favor, Thou hast made my mountain to stand strong. Thou didst hide Thy face, and I was troubled.* A Christian's life is, in some respect, like a courtier's who is near his prince. Upon his countenance or forbearance, all his comforts or discomforts depend. We may say of him what Mary spoke when she lost Christ, Luke 2:48, *Behold, thy father and I have sought thee sorrowing,* (i.e.

with a heavy heart).

But, how does it appear that this suspension of divine favor should occasion out doubtings? Thus:

1) God's favor is the greatest good. *Thy favor is life,* Psalm 30:5. He there expresses God's favor by that good which of us is most desirable. Nay, *Thy favor is better than life,* Psalm 63:3. Therefore, he cries out, Psalm 36:7, *O how excellent is Thy lovingkindness!* and prays, verse 10, *O continue Thy lovingkindness.* And Psalm 106: 4-5, *Remember me, O Lord, with the favor that Thou bearest unto thy people. That I may see the good of Thy chosen, etc.*

Now, the sensible absence of the greatest good must imprint the motions of greatest fear, suspicion, and trouble, as you may see in David, Psalm 77:3,7. *For now the glory seems to be departed from Israel.*

2) Again, in these times, nothing can comfort the soul or stay it without much difficulty. Our very graces will hardly uphold us. You know that if the king clouds his countenance, they are not the dignities conferred which will content us; they are not our revenues and possessions which will cheer us. So is it with us when God draws up His loving countenance: They are not our riches, or our gifts, or our graces, or our services, which can delight us. These do it, while in them, we see God's love shining towards us; but, if that draws back, these are all put to a strait. All is nothing to David while he is under this inquiry, *Will the Lord be favorable no more?* Psalm 77:7.

3) God seldom draws up His favor but for some unkindness on our part. Our sins (ordinarily) are the clouds which hide His face from us; they are the wall of separation: perhaps some great sin, as David's; perhaps some careless esteems of His speaking in His ordi-

nances; perhaps some slight passing by of His secret motions and counsels; as the church, Song of Solomon 5:2-3, *Open to me my sister, my love, my dove, my undefiled.* To which voice of Christ, how does the church demean herself? *I have put off my coat; how shall I put it on?* At length , though (verse 6) *I opened to my beloved, but my beloved had withdrawn himself, and was gone; my soul failed, &c.*

How can the soul but be greatly troubled when it has turned its day into night, and shut up that light which once it enjoyed to its great comfort and solace? *Woman, why weepest thou?* (said Christ to Mary, John 20:13). *Because* (said she) *they have taken away my Lord, and I know not where they have laid Him.* So may we justly weep when our sins have taken away our God from us in His comfortable favor, and we cannot easily regain Him and find Him.

4) These times of suspension ordinarily are times of trial, wherein God leaves the Christian to some notable combats and to the great exercises of grace; at which times corruptions and temptations will stir and, therefore, no marvel if they are times mixed with some fears and doubtings.

12. Another spring of doubtings is the crediting of Satan's testimony touching our estate when we rest upon his judgment and see our conditions through his informations. You know that objects are diversely represented to the eye; sometimes from themselves in their proper nature, as when a man sees a green color as it is; sometimes mediately, by other things, as when a green color is seen through a red glass. Now, it does not appear in its native color, but in the likeness of that through which it is perceived. So it is with our

spiritual estate.

Sometimes it is represented unto us as truly existing; and thus we shall see it when we look upon it and judge it by the work of God. Sometimes it is represented unto us not as it is, but as it appears in some corrupt and deceivable testimonies and reports unto us. As Joseph's chastity appeared to his master under the nature of abominable uncleanness, when he took the testimony of it from his filthy wife, so shall our most innocent and upright frame appear unto us to be nothing else but basest hypocrisy if we put the issue of it upon Satan's informations. As Satan has an art to color over the true condition of sinful bondage, keeping close and in covert the proper image, or rather deformity of it, so he has a delusion too, in hiding from our eyes the true powers of gracious sincerity, and fetching up to the judgment of all our weaknesses and present imperfections, with all former known evils with which he so totally possesses the mind that it can hardly see anything that good is in itself, or, if it does, yet it sees so much corruption and imperfection that it is ready almost to turn the scale and balance.

And here our crafty enemy does not cease, but, taking the advantage of a tender conscience, he exaggerates the large distance of this condition in which we now are, from that which God commands and expects, and has found in some of His righteous servants. In the citation of whose piety, he is not very sparing. By the consideration of their fullness and our own emptiness, we might the more easily suspect our condition and credit his relations; which, if we once do, *Bone Deus!* Into what labyrinths do we wind ourselves! Into what fears, into what doubts! We shall never set out to be-

lieve any promise but he checks us back with the
hollowness of our condition. We shall never set upon
any ordinance or duty but he foils us with suspicions
(at least) that all is in vain. "God will not bless and
prosper His ordinances unto such;" and, in those
ordinances, if any matter of bitterness or uncomfor-
tableness is delivered, he brings home that to us and
tells the soul, "This is your portion."

Now, where our estate rests upon a deceitful in-
former, where we take things as Satan makes them,
where we judge of sin as he pleads it, and of God's love
to us as he conveys it, and of God's promises as he in-
terprets them to us, and of our own graces and holy
temper, as he clears and evidences them unto us, there
can be nothing but jealousies, fears, distractions, and
daily doubtings in the heart.

13. Another spring may be some new risings of old
sins after humiliation and some singular assurance of
their pardon.

David gives a touch at this, I think (Psalm 25:7),
when he prays, *Remember not the sins of my youth, nor my
transgressions.* So does Job 13:26. *Thou writest bitter things
against me, and makest me possess the iniquities of my youth.*

It would trouble us to see a man rise up out of his
grave, who had been buried a long time, and now to
haunt us. So these sins, which we have long since
committed, and long since bewailed, and long since
renounced, and after long humiliations their discharge
has been obtained, to meet these sins (like an enemy
with a sword in his hand) with guilt in their faces and
countenances again, this will amaze the soul. It will ap-
pal it and startle it and make us more than once to sigh
and inquire, "Why is it so?"

Two things will now fall to question:

1) The reality of pardon. Where God said He pardons sin, there He says that He will remember it no more. But it seems He does remember it, else how does it come thus upon me as a debt not yet discharged, as a guilt not yet removed? And, if He does thus remember it against me, I much fear that as yet the book is not crossed, this sin is not pardoned; upon which something else may fall in: If this sin is not pardoned, perhaps the rest are not; and if this is risen up against me, how can I tell but all the rest may afresh set themselves in array and give a second charge upon my conscience too?

2) The reality of repentance. For where God calls for sound repentance (as Isaiah 1:16, *Wash you, make you clean; put away the evil of your doings from before Mine eyes; cease to do evil*), there God promises, verse 18, that *though your sins be as scarlet, yet they shall be as white as snow; and though they be red like crimson, yet they shall be as wool;* in which words are expressed a plain change of the sinful condition. Our sins shall not be what and as once they were.

Whereupon the soul misgives for its part. God will do what He has promised if I had done what I was enjoined. If my sins had been truly left, they would have been fully discharged; but now I possess them again in their guilt and, therefore, I exceedingly fear that I overtly discharged myself of them in my repentance. If Christ had slain them by His blood, or if I had drowned them by true sorrow and repentance, they could not thus revive in their guilt; but, I fear, I only skinned over these sores which I feel now to break out, or that I laid them asleep only, and not dead, because they awake upon me with such terror and clamor. And, if so, then there has been a long and fruitless vein of rotten hypocrisy in me. Whereas I had thought my work almost finished, I am as yet to begin again.

Beloved, this is a secret and piercing fountain of strong fears and doubtings, especially when the sins rise up and set on us afresh after a course of humiliation and some singular assurance of their pardon; and, yet, it is the case of many Christians incident unto them in their days of great losses, or sickness, or death.

14. Another spring or occasion may be some long silences in the conscience.

God (you know) has set in ourselves our Lawgiver, our Judge, and our Witness. Conscience sustains, and should discharge, the offices of all these. In a doubtful day it should clear our condition and witness for us against the testimony of Satan and our own fears; and, therefore, God has given unto it an excusing and comforting power, as you may see, Romans 2:15, *Their thoughts excusing one another, or accusing.* And 2 Corinthians 1:12, *Our rejoicing is this, the testimony of our conscience, that in simplicity and godly sincerity, etc.*

Here consider some particulars:

1. Concerning testimony.
2. Concerning our condition.

1. There is a three-fold testimony about our estate. One is from the spirit, which shines in the renewed heart by an unspeakable light and manifests unto it the things given unto it of God, and so seals and witnesses the truth and goodness of our particular interests in God and Christ according to the work of God.

Another is from faith, which testifies the interests of

the soul in that happiness which it finds revealed in the Word, for that which faith believes, by a direct act in the Word, it may testify of the same to the person by a reflexive act.

A third is from the conscience which, beholding the simplicity and godly sincerity of the heart, testifies unto it, against all opposition, that this blessed frame is in the soul, and this testimony being concordant with that of the Word, the soul is thereby greatly sustained, forasmuch as this is known before. A sincere temper is happy; and now conscience clearing that temper, the soul hereupon is much cheered.

2. Our condition falls under a three-fold consideration:

Sometimes under the accusations of conscience. Conscience speaks and testifies, but it is either that our hearts are totally base, sinful, and corrupt, or that, in such and such a particular, it is not right. It was not perfect, but sinful and degenerating.

Sometimes under the excuses of conscience; where conscience testifies, acquits, and speaks peace, either about the frame of the heart or rectitude of some particular action and course.

Sometimes under a neutral act or work of the conscience. The conscience (like Absalom to Am-non, 2 Samuel 13:22) speaks unto a person neither good nor bad. It does not accuse him, nor does it excuse him. It does not speak terror, nor does it speak peace. It does not charge any special guilt, nor does it give us any particular discharge of any.

Now this is the time of fears and doubts. I will show you why. Because:

1. A negative state does not satisfy a tender

Christian. It does not satisfy a tender soul that God does not look like an enemy unless He also looks like a friend; or that conscience does not check, but that it should excuse. It troubles us many times that, in our exemptions from trouble, we yet find no peace-speaker.

2. It gives suspicion of a neutral estate because conscience seems to behave itself as a neutral: neither against us nor for us. I call that a neutral state which is not eminently evil. It has some good in it and does some good, but is not so good as to be gracious. Therefore, the civil estate is a neutral one. It does not rise to be so bad as the worst, nor to be so good as the best people are. Now this estate, absolutely considered, is bad. It is an evil estate; it is an estate in which, if a man lives and dies, and goes not beyond it, he cannot be saved.

3. It may breed an expectation of the worst testimony of conscience, for withdrawments are sometimes the forerunners of some bitter intentions. It fell out ill with Saul when God withdrew himself from him. So, when conscience withdraws (perhaps my conscience has found matter against me), and as it does not now speak peace, so (perhaps shortly) it may speak bitter things unto me.

4. Nay, conscience is God's vice-regent. It is His deputy and, therefore, in the silences and withdrawments of it, we look through and fear the disposition of God Himself towards us because the servants ordinarily express the conceits, inclinations, and affections of their masters. And this is certain, that we, in angry conscience, behold always an angry God, and so, in a cheerful conscience, suspect a doubtful God. We ordi-

narily judge how God is towards us by what we find and feel conscience to be towards us. This is the glass in which we see His favors or frowns.

These are the springs of doubtings which I have enlarged in their opening unto you. It is likely there may be more than these. I could also deliver you more about the temporal estate, but that is out of our scope and compass now. It now remains that I descend to the closing up of these springs, to the cures and remedies of these doubtings, which is the last thing proposed.

Chapter 5

THE CURES AND REMEDIES OF DOUBTINGS

Here lies our next and greatest work; and, therefore, as physicians in this part are more cautious to administer things which are in their qualities most proper, and in their measures most convenient, so must we be in the healings and closings of the spiritual distempers of the soul. And, therefore, that this work may be happily performed, I shall (desiring God's grace to assist and bless) prescribe unto you: (I.) The particular cures which shall answer all those particular springs of doubtings before mentioned; then (II.) The general cures and remedies which may extend to the help of all or most of our doubtings, if time and leisure hold out.

THE PARTICULAR CURES

I. Natural corruption was the first spring of doubtings, and mortification is the first help and remedy. That is the disease and this is the cure. I may say that of our faith, which the apostle speaks of our persons, Romans 8:13, *If ye, through the Spirit, do mortify the deeds of the body, ye shall live.* The more our sins die in us, the more our faith will live in us. We are diseased men; take us in our best condition. And, you know, the more any disease loses of its strength, the more our health rises up and thrives. And so we are as a garden which has many plants and several weeds. The abating of these, the rooting up and killing of these, contributes the greater relief and strengthening to our plants.

The apostle (Hebrews 10.22) would have them to *draw near with a true heart in full assurance of faith.* He would have them to cast out their doubtings in their approaches unto God. He would have them to come with assurance, with a full assurance; to come so as verily to be persuaded of God's acceptance of them; not indifferently to come with, "Maybe I shall be accepted; maybe I shall not." This is a doubtful approaching, but what does he adjoin to this exhortation? Observe the next words, *Having your hearts sprinkled from an evil conscience.* As long as your hearts are evil, as long as conscience can charge you for entertained evil, you will be wavering and doubtful; but if your hearts were sprinkled, if the evil of sin were washed from them, then this might fully persuade you to come confidently unto God, for faith cannot well persuade if conscience can yet truly charge and condemn.

Therefore, said St. John, *If our hearts condemn us not, then have we confidence towards God.* If sin is mortified, if conscience finds no sin harbored but condemned, if it cannot condemn us for not condemning our sins, then we have confidence towards God. Then, if we come to God in prayer and ask anything of Him in the name of Christ, faith may confidently rest that God hears and will answer. *Whatsoever we ask, we receive of Him,* 1 John 3:22.

There are two effects of our sins:

1. They keep down our faith. *I am so troubled* (said David) *that I cannot look up* (See the place, Psalm 40:12). *Innumerable evils have compassed me about. Mine*

iniquities have taken hold on me, so that I am not able to look up. They are more that the hairs on my head; therefore my heart faileth me. You see here that his sins made his heart to fail, to misgive itself, and, like a heavy discharge that fell on his eyes, that he could not well look up. They are a hindrance to faith. Our natural inclination is a clog unto the spirit of faith; and, when faith would do some good for us, it ever, like a malicious person, throws in doubts and scruples, and breeds withholding arguments and reasonings against the truths and promises of God.

2. They make the encouragements of faith to be difficult; they keep off the things which would edge and quicken our faith. Peter said, in another case, *Depart from me, Lord, for I am a sinful man;* so says the heart here, "God will depart from me because of my sins; nor will He be gracious to me because of my sins; nor may I pitch upon His promises because of my sins."

Now, consider, if that which keeps down faith in respect of its proper inclination (for faith naturally bends upward) and in respect of its operation, that it cannot exercise itself without interruption, were remved, would not faith be higher? If the chains and bolts were off, if the rheum were dried, should we not walk better, should we not look better? Again, if the encouragements of faith were kept close to faith, if faith could see them and dwell upon them, would not our doubtings sink? Therefore, it is more than evident that our doubtings would sink if our natural corruption sank, if our sinful lusts sank, which breed those indispositions, those interruptions, those continual difficulties, unto our faith.

Faith would rise if its contrary abated. *Cast out this bondwoman and her son,* (said Sarah to Abraham), *for the son of this bondwoman shall not be heir with my son.* So I say, "Cast out this bondwoman and her son; cast out natural corruption and infidelity, that Isaac may be alone, that faith may be (as much as may be) alone, and then it will possess the promises (and the soul too) with more quietness."

But here the soul replies, "No question but doubtings would sink if sinful corruption fell; if the fountain decayed, the streams would lessen."

But, alas, who can mortify his sinful nature? What kind of mortifying of it is required? And what way may be taken to effect it?

I will briefly say something to each of these demands:

To the first, who can mortify his sinful nature? I answer, of himself, no man can. Naturally, he has neither will nor power thereto; but, as Chrysostom spoke in the business of repentance, you cannot turn yourself, but yet your God can turn you. That I say here in the business of mortifying. You cannot mortify your sins, but God can do it. He can do it for you. Though corruption is a spreading leprosy, He can heal it. Though it is a violent plague, He can cure it. God has put enough in Christ to save a sinner and, therefore, enough to heal a sinner. Remember one thing: in all commands, the duty is yours and the power is God's. He who commands you to mortify sin is ready enough with sufficient power to effect it, if He is sought unto. Nevertheless observe, by the way, that mortification may be effected two ways:

Passively, as when the Lord infuses holy principles

of grace, which are contrary, in their nature and virtue, to the nature and power of sin, working out sinful corruption by degrees.

Actively, as when the renewed and converted soul, by faith, successively applies and draws down the crucifying virtues of Jesus Christ. Though the mere natural man can do nothing to the mortification of sin, yet the renewed person, having received grace from God, is, by the help of God's spirit, to stir up the grace that is in him, and especially his faith; to trust on Jesus Christ for the further subduings and crucifyings of his sinful nature.

But now for the second demand. What kind of mortification is most requisite, so as, in more measure, to free the heart from doubtings? In a word, this: Be sure the mortifying is:

Radical. Lay the axe to the root. As all graces thrive most when their springs are quickened, so all sins decay most when their roots are mortified. Corrupt acts would fall quickly if the corrupt heart were more sanctified. The strength of sin is inward; there are the strongholds which need most to be cast down. By all means, set up a crucifying Christ in your bosom.

Impartial. It is true, one sin may trouble more than another, but it will be your wisdom to trouble all sin. Sins are chained together as well as graces, and one sin serves to help another, and the neglected sin may perhaps suddenly wound you and make you to stagger. The whole body of sin, every member of it, must be the object of your mortifying work. This will testify the truth of grace received, and the sincerity of your conscience, and consequently will remove many bottoms of fears and doubtings.

Diurnal, (i.e.) a daily work. Perhaps, sometimes, you are fervent in the work (when conscience is struck, or when affliction strikes you), but afterwards you are negligent, and then sin gets strength again. But, as you should live by faith daily, so you should die to sin daily. Watch your spirit; resist the motion of it; insist on divine promises; plead for the strength of Christ every day. You should so believe still as if you never yet had enough of Christ; and so live still, as if you were to live your last; and so mortify sin still, as you did at the first time God looked on you.

Special. If you would make your battle strong in any part, do it then against infidelity, and whatever upholds and contributes unto it. It is granted that the radical principle of your doubts is original sin, but then the immediate principle of it is remaining infidelity. Out of it, immediately, comes all your staggerings, reelings, questionings, and doubtings. That is (O weak believer) what disables your apprehension of the covenant, of Christ, of the promises, of your title. That is what perverts your judgment and mis-persuades it with cunning reasonings so that either you cannot discern the full truth of God's promises, or see prevailing reasons to persuade yourself that they belong to you.

Therefore, let your main care and work be to strike at unbelief. Be humbled much for it; beseech the Lord to cure you more and more of it, to remove the ignorance the covenant out of you and to cast down carnal and proud reasonings which give the lie to the way of God's free and full grace. This grace would have you to be first, and of yourself, that which you can never be without Christ; and to do and bring that which God never imposed on you to do or to bring. But He has told you plainly that the working of it in you belongs only to Himself, and He is also really and graciously willing to bestow upon you.

As for the third demand, what way you may take for the mortifying of all this sin, I answer:

Generally, touching all of it, insist in the ways on which already you are fallen. Did any virtue in the death of Christ (laid hold on by faith) heretofore help against sin? It will do so still. Did any love of God help you the more to hate sin? It will do so still. Did any assurance of a reconciled God in Christ, freely and abundantly pardoning you, weaken sin in you? It will do so still. Did solemn confessions of sin, self-judgings, special mournings, sufficiently help you with conquest of sins? They will do so still. Did the humble application of yourself to the ordinances of Jesus Christ (through which He is pleased to reveal His arm) confer any strength against your sins? It will help still. Did any holy fear, any tenderness in conscience, any declining of occasions, vehement wrestlings with God in prayer, serious meditation and consideration, close society with the saints, studies of further holiness, frequent reviewings of your condition, and renewings of covenant with your God in His strength, holy watchings, resistings of the first births of sin; did these, any of these, all of these, or any other spiritual course besides these, cause your sinfulness to be vile unto you, to be abhorred by you, to be cast down in your judgment, to be cast out in your affections, to be cast off in your life? Go on with these, and sin will then be more and more mortified, and doubts will be more and more weakened. The more that your conscience is thus sprinkled from dead works, the more shall you be able to draw near unto God in assurance of faith.

Particularly for the mortifying of remaining infidelity, do three things:

First, study exactly the covenant of grace, in the author of it, foundation of it, matters contained in it, and all the adjuncts and terms of graciousness, suitableness, fullness, faithfulness, appertaining to it.

Second, study Jesus Christ thoroughly; know Him distinctly in the person of a Mediator, offices, effects, and works.

Third, do much meditation in these; abound in prayer that God, in particular, would cause you by faith to set your seal unto them. But more of this will follow in answering some other causes of doubtings.

II. The second spring was weakness and imperfection in faith. The cure and remedy is to perfect and strengthen faith. Put more strength, more growth, more ripeness into faith, and your doubtings will be less. The more purely the fire burns, the less smoke it has; and, when the light and heat of the sun are greatest, then the clouds and misty vapors are fewest.

Faith and doubtings are like a pair of scales, where the weight of the one bears away the other. The disciples, I remember, prayed, *Lord, increase our faith,* and so did he of whom you heard in Mark 9, *Lord, help my unbelief.*

You will say, "No man can deny that, if his faith had more strength, then his heart should have less doubting, but how may that be done? How may faith be strengthened?"

I answer:

1. God, who gave faith, can strengthen it; for every

grace depends upon Him not only for birth, but also for complement. His strength must lead us on from strength to strength, from faith to faith. He who is the Author is also the Finisher of it; and, therefore, if you would have a strong faith, you should go to a strong God and beg Him, "Lord, increase my faith. My knowledge is dim; lighten that candle. Open my eyes yet more, that I may see Thy truths. My assents, many times, are shaking, but establish and confirm my heart in Thy truths. My embracings, applications, are very trembling, broken, and interrupted; but guide my eyes to look upon my Savior. Guide my hand to lay hold on Him; enable my will and affections to embrace all the goodness of Thyself, of Thy Christ, of Thy work."

It is God's method to lay in (at the first) weak faith that we might beg for more faith and give Him the honor of all. If we had strong faith at first, He should not hear us; but He dispenses it by degrees so that, in all our gettings, and in all our victories over doubtings, His strength may have the glory. Therefore, go to God and say, "Lord, I would have more faith, and Thou would have me to perfect it; but all perfection is in Thee, and I cannot, by my mere strength, ripen what Thou givest, but Thou canst water what Thou plantest. Though it is sown a weak body; though faith, at first, is but as a grain of mustard seed, yet Thou canst cause it to blossom and to spread itself into a high measure. Therefore, Thou who alone canst do it, do it for Thy weak servant. Thou must take charge of Thine own graces; and, if Thou givest my faith more strength, my believing will bring Thee in the more glory."

2. Studying Christ and the promises more will bring more strength and perfection to faith. It is with the

Christian as it is with the scholar; let the scholar study more the objects of knowledge, and then his knowledge will grow to be more large. So, let the Christian study more the matters of faith, and his faith will rise to be more full. Hence the apostle prays that the Ephesians, 3:19, *might know the love of Christ, that they might be filled with all the fullness of God,* and verse 17, *that Christ might dwell in their hearts by faith, that so they might be able* (verse 18) *to comprehend, with all saints, what is the breadth, and length, and depth, and height.* What the prophet spoke of perishing, we may say of fainting and doubting, "My people doubt for want of knowledge."

If we knew the nature of our Redeemer more, how holy and compassionate and helpful it would be. If we knew the offices of our Savior, how absolute they are in removing our guilt, in conquering our corruptions, in making way for us to the Father, in speeding our suits and requests; if we knew how fully He stands for us, He died for us, He intercedes for us, how willing He is yet to be more applied by us and possessed of us, we would believe more and doubt less. What the Psalmist speaks of God is true of Christ: *They that know Thy name, will put their trust in Thee.* Yet, take a caution in your studying of Christ. Study Him as God reveals Him, otherwise your doubts will stick upon you. If a man studies his sins in his own way, in a natural way, he shall neither rightly see them nor yet be freed from them. So, if men study Christ their own way, if they will have Him to be such a One as their fearful hearts would make Him to be, and not such a Savior as God has manifested Him to be, then, not conceiving of Christ as He is, they shall be, and remain still, as they were.

3. Be in the ways of strength. There are ways in

which God reveals His arm. His arm is that which
strengthen us, and His arm is revealed in His ordinances; for God does not call us, nor change us, nor
strengthen us, nor save us, without means. He who is
too good for the ordinances will ever be too weak in
his faith. A child which cannot stand when it is born
may yet go by the use of the breasts; but that person
who is weak and wants strength, if he does not feed,
will abate more and, ere long, lack life itself. This is a
truth. A new Christian is sometimes full, and a full
Christian is always weak; for our spiritual life is like our
natural life, both of which are within us, yet neither of
them do rise but from something without us. What the
impotent person spoke, John 5:11, *He that made me
whole, the same said unto me, Take up thy bed and walk,*
that we affirm of God's ordinances. Those means
which make us good can make us better; they made us
live, and they can make us walk. They gave faith; they
brought the hand which set the plant, and they can enlarge faith. They bring the showers which water that
plant. For:

    1) They evidence Christ more, and open and
        unfold the promises (which are the stays of
        our faith) more.

    2) They enervate or weaken, and scatter the
        grounds of our fears and doubtings, and
        exceedingly suppress the reasonings and
        powers of unbelief.

    3) They clear the understanding, and so keep
        open the way for faith to God and Christ.

    4) They instill a secret and drawing virtue; they
        excite, quicken, and persuade. Ergo:

4. Fourth, let faith know its privileges and then it

will grow more strong. Faith would do more if it knew all that it might do. Assuredly, we should have more confidence if we knew our royalties. Believers are more to God than the most immediate servants are to a prince. All the subjects of a prince have some privileges, yet theirs are greatest who are in the nearest service. Now none is nearer to God than believers. See 1 Peter 2:9, *Ye are a chosen generation, a royal priesthood, and holy nation, a peculiar people.* Nay, 2 Corinthians 6:18, *Ye shall be my sons and daughters, saith the Lord Almighty.* And these have those privileges which the servants have not. They who descended from the blood of Abraham had more privileges than others; and have not they greater who come from the blood of Christ?

The priests of the law had singular exemptions, and kings, of all men, are most highly privileged. Do you think believers come short who are not profane, nor civil, not typical priests, but royal priests? Who are not priests only, nor kings only, but both kings and priests, a royal priesthood? Who are a holy nation, a peculiar people, (i.e.) a people of treasure, such by whom only God gets something?

"O" (say many weak believers), "the Lord does not respect nor love us." No. Does not God love those whom (out of His mere love) He has chosen? Does not God respect the descent and generation of Christ? Those who come of His blood, who come from Christ and are born of God, are surely beloved of God.

But the world, all men discountenance us and regard us not. You are kings in God's account; you have the royal ointment, even the spirit of grace; the royal garment, even the righteousness of Christ; the royal attendance, even the angels of God ministering unto you. You have a kingdom which consists in righteousness, peace, and joy, Romans 14:17. Cannot this stir up faith?

We are, oftentimes, afraid to come before God. Do we fear access? Are you not believers, and are not believers the priests of God, and are not priests privileged by their calling to come before God? *The priests might enter in when none else might.* And is not Jesus Christ the altar upon which we tender all our sacrifices and services to God, and is it not the altar that sanctifies the gift? Matthew 23:19. The apostle said, Galatians 5:1, that *Christ has gotten us a liberty.* And Ephesians 2:13, that *we are made nigh by the blood of Christ.* And Hebrews 10:19, that *we may have boldness top enter into the holiest by the blood of Jesus.*

If, therefore, we once thoroughly knew what privileges the first-born have, the sons of God have, the generation of Christ have, the priests of God have, the purchased by Christ have; if we knew the grants of favor, free accesses, and singular acceptances with God in and through Christ, O how might we keep down our fears and our doubtings, and singularly encourage our faith to run, and with fullest eagerness to embrace our God, our Christ, our promises!

There are other means for the perfecting of faith, as experiences, observation, etc., which I have touched long since; and our divines are plentiful this way, and therefore I will spare y ou.

III. The third spring of doubtings was the study of the life of sense; the remedy of which is, the keeping of it down. If you will keep off doubtings, you must keep down sense and feeling. *Blessed* (said Christ to

Thomas, John 20:29) *are they that have not seen, and yet have believed.*

If a man thinks that Christ is not mine unless I handle Him; and God is not mine unless I see Him; and grace is not mine unless I feel it; he will be forever full of doubts and fears.

For the helping of which, consider these things:

1. Sense is not a fit judge of our condition. It cannot report our estate but by what it feels; but the spiritual estate is not always under feeling. We should be good and bad, found and lost, cheerful and sorrowful, many times in one day, nay, in one hour, if that sense gave sentence on our condition.

Beloved, think well on this. How can sense reach unto the times of desertion, unto the times of want, unto the times of indisposition, unto the times where faith expresses no acts but such as are pure and clear, and only grounded upon the promises? In these abstracted times, sense finds nothing to speak to us, to evidence for us, for God holds off, and wants hold up, and dullness holds in, and we have nothing but a word of promise (all other things seem to fail and forsake) to sustain and retain us.

2. The spiritual course, many times, goes against our sense and, therefore, sense must be kept down. You know that Abraham, against hope, believed in hope, Romans 4:18. Faith and sense are, many times, at a contradiction; faith will believe what sense perceives not, and, what our sense perceives, that same our faith will not believe but the contrary. *Though He kill me, yet will I trust in Him,* said Job. And Abraham believed his son's safety in the sacrificing of him; and we our immortality, notwithstanding our death and corruption.

This is very certain, that when we feel corruptions living, faith will believe them to be dying; and, when we feel ourselves in trouble, faith will then believe our comforts and deliverances. Faith usually (I do not say always) believes the contraries unto sense. For sense goes our way and faith goes God's way. Sense allows and sets itself a time, and faith is content to receive and take God's times. Sense moves upon what appears, and faith upon what is not yet. Sense looks downward and faith looks upward. Sense sustains itself by something within us, and faith sustains itself by something without us, Psalm 27:3, so Habakkuk 3:17-18. So Isaiah 8:17, *I will wait upon the Lord that hideth His face from the house of Jacob, and I will look for Him.* Isaiah 50:10, *Who is he that walketh in darkness and has no light? Let him trust in the name of the Lord, and stay upon his God.*

3. Sense or feeling is not *medium credendi*, but *fructus fidei*: It is not the ground of believing, but a fruit of faith. Take feeling in the most excellent parts of it, as in assurance, and joy, and peace; these are not antecedents to faith, but consequents of it. What is that? That is, a man does not have these first, and then faith for or from these; but he has faith first and these afterward.

Why do you not believe? "If I had assurance that God were my God, that Christ were my Christ, and the promises were mine, I would." But say, is the Word or your assurance the ground of faith? And would you have the fruit before the tree, or your safety before you lay your hand on the rock? If you would have assurance, you must then believe; for the sweetness of assurance flows from that faith, which, by believing, feeds of Christ. So, if you would have joy, believe; for true joy does not prevent, but attends believing.

We are, oftentimes, troubled by our own pride and folly. God sets us away to believe, and we will follow our own way. He gives unto us His work of promise to ground our believing, and we will have our sense to be the ground. I dare say here what Abraham spoke to the curiosity of Dives, who would have some to be sent from the dead that his brethren might believe, to whom Abraham thus replies, *If they hear not Moses and the prophets, neither will they be persuaded though one rose from the dead,* Luke 16:31. So say I. If men will not believe because God has promised, neither will they believe if sense should stand up and speak; for we have more reason to suspect our own testimony than to distrust God's invitation and promise. You will reply, "This testimony of sense in assurance is God's own answer and, therefore, if we had it, it would the more settle our faith." I answer:

1) God's testimonies are indeed of a settling and quieting virtue, whether they are the evidencing of our present interests in Him or special answerings of our present desire.

2) But then know that you must first put to your seal and hand of faith before He delivers over to you the assuring evidences. I never knew any Christian could be answered without faith, or took comfort in that which yet he did not believe; for, though it is the favor of God which properly comforts, nevertheless it does not actually comfort unless faith has taken in that favor.

"But are not former experiences (which are nothing else but sensible feelings) grounds to future belief? Did not David remember the days of old?"

I answer, "True." Experiences are good encouragements to the future acts of faith, but the Word of God is still the ground of faith. They are not intrinsical grounds, but extrinsical motives.

You may consider the experiences, either in things granted and performed or in the manner of their performance. You have had God's favor; you have had an answer, but how did you obtain them? Was it not by believing? Was it not by waiting upon some good word of promise? Your enjoying of them did not prevent your believing the word of promise, but believing that the word of promise let in and brought unto your soul that sweet and gracious experience; and, therefore, your experience was not the ground heretofore, nor is it now. Only as far it serves as a singular furtherance to faith, that God, on whom heretofore you believed, and from whom, in believing, you received such gracious helps and answers, will again (He being the same forever, and His promises being yea and amen) by further believing on His work, renew His gracious goodness and merciful favor unto your soul.

IV. A fourth spring was the restraining of faith, the curbing of it in its work and occasions. Now the remedy of this is to gibe way unto faith; give it scope; let it do its whole service. As the apostle said of patience, James 1:4, *Let patience have her perfect work,* so let faith. Do not restrain it, and then you shall be stayed; you shall be freed. The workings of one contrary restrain the other. Therefore, Christ checks His disciples for their anxieties, for their carkings and solicitudes, and would have them to let their faith loose to see a Father who would provide, Matthew 6:32. They had poverty, or feared it; their wants came in, and losses, and so their fears came in, and their thoughts. But how should they cast them out? Thus, if faith believed helps, as well as impatience finds wants, if they would give way to faith to believe God's providing, as well as sense to see the world abridging and ebbing, they would not have been so full of thoughts. *Shall He not much more clothe you of little faith?* Verse 30.

But for further help in this point, consider:

1. In any occurrence, faith may be our agent; it can deal for us, because:

1) Our temporal life is by faith.

2) The temporal promises which reach over all the external condition are the bottom of faith. Hence it is said, Habakkuk 2:4, *The just shall live by his faith.* When we have no other help, yet faith can be our staff. When we have no other feeding, yet faith can be our bread. It can negotiate for the soul; it can make repair to God and singularly solace and sustain the soul in His work of promise.

Suppose a man's means begin to shrink, his condition is drawing thin. He is near to want; at such a time this man may keep down his doubts and tearing thoughts if he will give faith a scope to work. *I will never leave thee nor forsake thee,* Hebrews 13:5. Here is a promise now, and here is plenty enough to faith; and faith (if it may have its perfect work) will sustain you against all doubtings.

Do you say, "I shall be left."?

"You shall not," says faith.

"Not now, perhaps, for yet I have something."

"Nay, never," says faith, "for you have a continual God, and He has promised a continual help. You would be a free man if faith were free; for faith will not leave God, and God will not fail faith. And why should you fail when faith holds up your heart, and God holds up your faith? So it is for any cross and trouble; there is no burden this way, but faith may be a shoulder to ease us. As long as there is a promise to bear up faith, faith will have strength to bear off the disquietudes of our troubles.

"I do not know what to do," says the person.

"No?" says faith. "Is not the Lord good, *a stronghold in the day of trouble,* and *does not He know them that trust in Him?*" Nahum 1:7.

"But troubles are renewed and come again; and, though I was delivered heretofore, yet now I fear."

"Fear?" says faith. "No reason for that." See a notable place, Job 5:17. *Happy is the man whom God correcteth.* If a man has wounds, it is well for him to have a searching plaster; and, if a man has a full stomach, it is well for him if he has a potion; and, if his spirits putrify, it is well for him to be let blood.

Verse 18. *For He makes sore, and binds up; He wounds, and His hands make whole.*

Verse 19. *He shall deliver you in six troubles, yea, in seven. There shall no evil touch you.*

There is nothing new to God or difficult. Though our troubles are grievous to us, yet their deliverance is easy to God, and faith can find a harbor for every storm. Yea, give faith but its scope and it will conclude present helps from former deliverances. And the escape out of old troubles shall ensure faith in the new. *He who has delivered, does, and will still deliver,* 2 Corinthians 1. God does not alter, neither in His truth, nor in His goodness, nor in His power, although our conditions vary. The temptation may be new, and the affliction may be new, but God is still the same; and the promises are still the same; and faith can make use of one God to conquer twenty temptations, and one promise to bear up against many afflictions.

2. In every occurrence there is a providence, and the issues depend on it. If Satan tempts, if afflictions, crosses, losses, and contempts befall us, there is a providence to permit them, to order them, to direct them, to restrain them; and, if we gave faith a scope to work upon that providence, we would not be so full of doubts.

1) For Satan indeed tempts and suggests, but he cannot do this when he pleases. He must ask permission of God to touch Job in any way; and, when he does tempt, the issue does not depend upon his malice. The Lord looks on and subministers marvelous strength and makes His servants to pray earnestly, hear earnestly, and apply His promises, and He will deliver. We look upon Satan and not upon God. We look upon strong temptations, but we do not look upon mighty assistances. We consider our own weaknesses, but do not consider God's omnipotence; we think how unable we are, but not how able God is. We find no deliverance, and do not give faith its perfect work to believe that God will find a way to conquer for us. If faith did but dwell upon God's providence in this, how He suffers Satan to buffet us, and how His grace is sufficient for us, and how His power will be made manifest in weakness, how He has delivered, and in our very resistance delivers us, and has promised to bruise Satan under our feet, we would not doubt. We would not gratify Satan with fears of fainting, but resist him stead-

fastly by encouraging ourselves in our God.

2) For our crosses and losses, there is a providence in them. God is in all our troubles and wants. His wisdom is there as well as His goodness. "O, how shall I be delivered?" How? Let faith work, and that will tell you how. "Why should I thus be troubled?" Why? Let faith work and that will tell you. It is in His very faithfulness, said David, and *It is good for me that I am afflicted.* No child of God thus! Nay, let faith work, and it will clear all, that a good condition is not exempted from afflictions, and that, though God had one Son without sin, yet He had no son without sorrow.

3) Our encouragements are more than our discouragements, and our helps exceed our oppositions; therefore, faith is not to be restrained.

The prophet healed his servant's doubtings, 2 Kings 6:16, *Fear not, for they that be with us are more than they that be with them* . This is what Christ said to His perplexed and doubting disciples about those exigencies and casualties to which they were exposed. *Fear not, little flock, it is your Father's pleasure to give you a kingdom.* Do not be so disquieted, so anxious for your lives, for your safeties. Though you are a flock, and a little flock, and the wolves are many, yet let the worst come to the worst; you shall have a kingdom.

Oppose that to this, and you need not doubt and fear. So said John, I John 4:4, *Ye are of God, little children and have overcome them, because greater is He that is in you, than he that is in the world.*

Once more, we hear St. Paul, Romans 5:20, *Where sin abounded, grace did much more abound.* And, verse 21, *As sin reigned unto death, so grace reigns through righteousness unto eternal life by Jesus Christ our Lord.*

So again for outward troubles, Isaiah 41:14, *Fear not, thou worm Jacob.* You are a weak creature, a contemptible creature, a worm, yet you are Jacob and, therefore, do not fear, *for I will help thee, saith the Lord.* Though Jacob is weak, yet the God of Jacob is strong. So for outward losses, 2 Chronicles 25:9, said Amaziah to the man of God, *But what shall we do for the hundred talents which I have given to the army of Israel?* The man of God answered, *The Lord is able to give thee much more than this.* From all which we see, that faith has the better grounds to rest on.

There are more with faith than against it; for none can be against it except the evil creatures; and He who is for it is the mighty Creator. All His power, His goodness, His Christ, His Spirit, and His work of truth is for it. He is greater than all so that faith may have singular matters to work upon in all occurrences. It is on the better side, and on the greater side, on that side which will carry it and bear down the contrary. Satan is against me; but greater is He (that Spirit of Christ) in me than he that is in the world. Sin is against me, but greater is Christ who is for me; grace has much more abounded. Men, in their power, are against me, but greater is that Almighty God, before whom the nations are but as the drop of the bucket and lighter than a dust in the balance. Troubles are upon me; but my comforts are greater than my sorrows, and the glory which I expect infinitely exceeds the trouble which I suffer. Wants are upon me, but my supplies are exceeding. I have a provident Father; and, though I have not a large portion on earth, yet I have a sure kingdom in heaven.

Beloved, if we would but often consider this, that

faith is still on the better, on the surer side, we would
quit all our doubtings. We would not fear what man
can do unto us, what Satan can do unto us; our own infirmities would not disable us, nor afflictions, for still
faith falls to the surest party and, therefore, gives it
scope. Faith pitches upon no weak causes, upon no
weak helps, upon no weak stays. It stays upon the name
of the God of Jacob.

O how might faith outface the greatest oppositions,
and trample under all our affronts and losses and
doubts, if we did let it get out its encouragements; if we
could once come with faith to be persuaded indeed
that they who are for us are more than they who are
against us!

Brethren, in our spiritual combats, we have the better cause and the better strength; what help heaven
can afford, we have. Therefore, in all our distresses, let
us hearten ourselves and encourage our faith. Let us
(as Jehu in another case) look up and say, *Who is on my
side, who?* and then we may even say what the Psalmist
spake, Psalms 124:1, *If it had not been the Lord who was on
our side, now may* (the believer) *Israel say, 2. If it had not
been the Lord, etc. 7. Our soul is escaped as a bird out of the
snare, etc. 8. Our help is in the name of the Lord, etc.*

**V. A fifth spring of doubtings is special and particu-
lar sins after conversion.** These, like a strong disease,
shake the very heart and spirit of the Christian and
stagger him on every side. Like a cloud, they ford up
all our comfortable communion with God. Like a dead
fly, they fall in all our services. *If thou dost ill, sin lies at
the door,* said God to Cain. And so you shall find that
special sins, after conversion, greatly interrupt us in

our approaches and in our confidences.

Now, the way to cure this spring is:

1. To renew our sorrows, to set upon the fountain. David did so after his great sins, and so did Peter. The one did *water his couch,* and *his tears were his meat day and night,* and the other *went out and wept bitterly.* Bitterness of sorrow (you read of it in Zechariah 12:10) imports:

1) An anguish of spirit. As David said for his Jonathan, *My soul is distressed for thee,* so here, the fallen Christian is distressed for sinning thus against his God, for losing his God. There is oftentimes a very tearing and renting in the soul.

2) A sensible fullness of grief. As Joseph was full of compassion, and his bowels could hold no longer upon the oration of Judah, so the fallen Christian is full of holy meltings. His heart is ready to break and, like a full vessel, it must have vent.

Many a time he must, and does, consider this vile sin, and gets himself alone to pour out his grieved heart before the Lord, and shames himself before Him, and confesses, with confusion of face, his treacherous and unworthy dealing against his God.

There is, you know, a natural sorrow, as for the loss of children; and a political sorrow, as was for the good King Josiah; and there is a spiritual sorrow, which is for our sins. This must now be exceedingly renewed, and you may raise it by consideration of mercy. "O Lord, what have I done? Why have I done this? Thou showed me mercy in opening my eyes, in changing my heart, in calling me to holiness, in pardoning my former sins; yet, after all this, I have sinned against Thee. I have wounded Thy heart, dishonored Thy name, turned

Thy grace into wantonness, lost Thy favor, broke my peace, injured my Christ, grieved Thy spirit, turned away Thine ear, given advantage to Satan, and deserved forever to sit in darkness."

Beloved, if you find your hearts unhumbled, you shall find your hearts still to be unbelieving. For besides that, great sins are great provocations to our gracious God; they are also (till we are humbled for them) great impediments to faith. Faith cannot do service for us, it cannot uphold us, it cannot bring a comforting promise unto our hearts, until our hearts are humbled for our sin. God comforts none but mourners; and faith cannot fall in with Him until our hearts fall out with ourselves. And here take heed that you are not slight and too quick. If you are, you shall have your doubtings again. God seldom or never speaks easy peace after a great sin. If you skin up a sore, it will break out again. If your sorrows are not deep and sound, your fears will be fresh and multiplied. But let them be pious and serious, and then the soul will, after a while, recover itself, and plead and find mercy with God, and be able to answer and silence all the doubtful reasonings which will rise against faith in its wonted communions and applications.

"But," you will say, "if we should sorrow thus, yet we should still doubt of mercy and God's favor."

I answer:

a) You have now to answer your doubtings: "True, I did sin thus, but I have truly grieved for this sin; and, though I might not apply mercy because I sinned, yet now I may because I am grieved."

b) See God's disposition to Ephraim, Jeremiah 31:18, *I have surely heard Ephraim bemoaning himself, etc.*

Verse 19, *I was ashamed, yea, even confounded, because I did bear the reproach of my youth.* But then, verse 20, *Is Ephraim my dear son? Is he a pleasant child? for since I spake against him, I do earnestly remember him still; therefore my bowels are troubled for him, I will surely have mercy upon him, saith the Lord.*

Though God is offended with our sins, yet He is delighted in our sorrows; and nothing melts Him more than to see us come melting before Him. The mournful behavior of Joseph's brethren moved Him, and the returning prodigal's falling down to his father and crying out went to the heart of Him; and it is not without cause that David prays, *Regard my tears that fall;* and, *Are not my tears registered?* and, *Put Thou my tears into Thy bottle.* Melting tears melt a tender God and Father.

2. To renew our repentance, in which I would comprehend both detestations and forsakings. These sins must be made very hateful to the soul. You must embitter them; you must purge out all the sweetness of them, all the liking of them; nay, you must set upon them as on things most abominable. Hence that phrase of *loathing your abominations,* Ezekiel 36.

St. John, Revelation 2:5, advised decayed Ephesus to *remember from whence she was fallen,* and, *to repent.* Beloved, this is not a condition to stay in; this water is deep, and drowning is possible if we lie in it. But, if we rise out of our sins, then our doubtings will fall. It is with our consciences as it is with water in a pot. If you put no fire under it, it is quiet; but, if you kindle a fire, the water will boil and bubble; it has no quiet. So, though conscience is quiet and kind, and molests us not, if yet fire come under, if any notable sin come in and kindle in the heart; now come the boilings, now come the fears and doubts of the soul. And, in these tumblings, the way to cease them is to remove the fire, and then you shall see how the water grows to a stillness again and, by degrees, leaves fuming. So will our souls come to a pacified temper, to a settledness, if once our sins are removed. Leave the sins and, ordinarily, the doubts will leave the sinner; for, as sin is our unquiet sea, so repentance is our secure harbor. Any known sin unrepented of still puts in and enlivens doubts in us; but repentance plucks out the venom and the rage. An amended child comes again before his father, and a reformed Christian and a penitent may yet be confident.

3. Sue out a special assurance. You may see by David's disposition, after his special sins, that a general acquittance would not serve the turn. For special sins, you must sue out special assurance of pardon. Your consciences will never be quiet, else (nay, this will not satisfy you) they are pardonable; they are such as do not exclude you out of proclamation. Your consciences will never be quiet until God speaks peace, until He puts His seal to acquit you of particular sins. Sin will rise; it will lie uppermost; you shall feel it so it will fly in your face. It will come up in serious times until you repent of it and sue your discharge. Therefore, be earnest with the Lord for pardon of it, for a special acquittal. If the Lord Jesus sealed His blood upon your heart, your doubtings would cease.

"But," you will say, "there is now no hope. Though we should grieve, though we should repent, though we should sue for pardoning mercy, there is now no hope, for these are sins after conversion, and they are great ones too. And, besides, we find no particular promise to ease our souls."

Let me answer this doubt fully, for it is a folded one; there are many in it. Consider therefore:

1) The promise of pardon is indefinite to repentance; and I beseech you to mark this point. God does not simply say, "I will pardon sins," but "if men repent and forsake sins, they shall have mercy." So again, in promising pardon to repentance, He does not promise it respectively and conditionally, but absolutely and fully.

What is that? That is, God does not say, "If you repent of such or such sins, then you shall have pardon"; but He says simply and absolutely, "If you repent." So that, let the sins be never so great, never so many, yet if they are sins of which you now truly repent, they are assuredly pardoned, Isaiah 55:7, *Let the wicked forsake his way, and the unrighteous man his thoughts, and let him return unto the Lord, and He will have mercy upon him; and to our God, for He will abundantly pardon.* Here you see a promise of abundant pardon to be made unto the penitent. Though he has had thoughts, though he has had ways, yet, if he forsakes them, the Lord will pardon and show mercy.

Again, because that pardon is promised to actual repentance indefinitely, therefore, let the sinner be what he will, let him be a person who was not converted before, or let him be a person already converted, yet if he begins true repentance, or renews his true repentance, shall be pardoned. And the reason is it is not sin simply in such an estate which God pardons, but it is sin repented of which God promises to pardon.

Therefore, if an evil man, whose life has been a

course of sins, repents and leaves his sins, he shall have mercy; or, if a good man fall accidentally into sin, upon his repentance, he may confidently plead out God's promises of pardon, for he shall have mercy upon his repentance, as you may see in Proverbs 28:13, *He that forsakes his sins shall find mercy.* Ezekiel 18:32, *Turn yourselves, and live.* See verses 21, 22, *If the wicked will turn from all his sins, they shall not be mentioned unto him.*

Whence we may infer that, if God will forgive His enemies, He will then (upon the same repentance) forgive His children. If a king will pardon a returning traitor, will he not receive then a returning son? It was a pious speech of St. Chrysostom, " If He promiseth grace unto us when we are sinning, what then will He confer on us if we are repenting?"

2) Christ is of great virtue still, and is as able to put away the sins after conversion as well as before. Therefore is He called *the same, yesterday, today, and forever.* And the apostle reasons it in Romans, *If when we were enemies, we were reconciled to God by the death of His Son; how much more, being reconciled, shall we be saved by His life?* We must think of the pacification by Christ, of the atonement, of the propitiation, of the satisfaction, not as confined to any one sin or to any one state, but in respect of its sufficiency, reaching over both estates and all the sins in both. What is that? That is, the death of the Lord Jesus was not only to reach the sins you committed in your unconverted estate, and the rest afterward in your converted estate, you are to satisfy for by your own power some other way. What is this but that popish leaven, that self-justification, those human satisfactions? What is this but to divide our salvation between Christ and ourselves? What is this but to

restrain either the sufficiency or the efficacy of His death?

No, Christ is unto us, in respect of sins before and sins after conversion, as the Lord was to the Israelites, a pillar of cloud and a pillar of fire. Jesus Christ is a cloud in the day (in the time of conversion) to cover our sins upon our repentance, and a pillar of fire by night (for the times of former darkness), upon our repentance, to consume away our sins.

The difference of our estates in no way adds or diminishes the strength and efficacy of His death. His blood can cry as loud now as before, and is no less effectual to get pardon for our falls in the way, than for our sinnings when we were not in the way, as is evident in the sins of Paul before his conversion; for Christ is our continual Mediator and ever-living Intercessor.

"But," you will reply, "these sins cut off all our interest in Christ, and all relation and, therefore, there is no hope now."

I answer, "Though the comfortable interest is cut off until the time of sound repentance, yet the radical interest is not." As the leprous person was barred the use of his house until he was cleansed, yet he was not barred the title and right of his house; and, therefore, you may, upon your repentance, sue unto the Lord, by the blood of your Savior, the pardon of these sins.

3. The Lord is merciful still unto repentant persons. You shall read in Psalms 136 that His mercy is set down twenty-six times with the adjunct of everlastingness, *His mercy endureth for ever.* And Psalms 86:5, *Thou, Lord, art good, and ready to forgive, and plenteous in mercy unto all them that call upon Thee.* So, verse 13, *Great is Thy mercy towards me.* And verse 15, *Thou, O Lord, art a God*

full of compassion, and gracious, longsuffering, and plenteous in mercy and truth. So, Micah, 7:18-19, *Who is a God like unto Thee, that pardoneth iniquity, and passeth by the transgression of the remnant of his heritage? He retaineth not His anger for ever, because He delighteth in mercy. He will turn again, He will have compassion on us, He will subdue our iniquities, and Thou wilt cast all their sins into the depths of the sea.*

Mercy is not strange unto God. It is His nature; it is His delight, and repentance will not be hid from His eyes if it is not hid from our hearts. He calls us to repent and causes us to repent, that He might show us His mercy and the everlastingness of His mercy.

VI. A sixth spring of doubtings is indisposition unto or about spiritual duties, whence we fear the truth of grace, which is active and lively, and doubt our acceptance with God by reason of our dullness and deadness. For the curing of this, consider:

1. That dullness in holy duties is possibly incidental to men truly sanctified. Beloved, there is a great difference between a dead heart and a dull heart. That heart is properly termed dead which lacks a living spring and, therefore, spiritual duty is contrary unto it. It has a secret aversion to holy services; it does not care for holy prayer. There is not only an indifference as to whether the work is done, but a determinate dislike and positive unwillingness to the same, a nillingness or nolition; whence arises that shuffling carriage in wicked men to find diverting occasions and arguing reasonings against the strictness and spiritualness of duty.

But, again, that heart is properly termed dull which

has in it a living spring, but does not have a lively oper-ation. *The spirit is willing,* said Christ; there the spring was open, *but the flesh is weak.* There the operation was narrow. The Christian may say with David, *My heart, O Lord, is ready; my heart is prepared;* and, as Paul, *I would do good,* and *I delight in the law of God after the inward man.* But yet, said he, *I find a law that, when I would do good, evil is present with me;* and *I see another law in my members, warring against the law of my mind.* So, in the Galatians, *The flesh lusteth against the spirit, etc. and these are contrary one to the other, so that ye cannot do the things that ye would.* You would do, but you cannot do; you cannot always do the work you would do, and you can-not do it in such a manner as you would do it.

You know that a full vessel which has a narrow neck cannot send out the waters so speedily, not so fully; and a sick man, who would fetch more than a turn about his chamber, cannot do that sometimes. If he does, it is with extreme wearisomeness, not of his mind, but of his body; or, as a lusty and able man es-caped out of prison with a great chain about his leg, he would run away, but the chain hinders and vexes him so that it indisposes him in the motion. In like manner is it, many times, with good people. The heart and the will is bent; it is resolved for prayer, for hearing, etc. But, then, there is a chain that clogs them; there is a spiritual weakness, there is flesh in them as well as spirit, and this dulls them. This indisposes them about the doing, about the exercise of their intentions and desires.

Therefore, let us take heed of denying or conclud-ing the absence of grace from the infirmity of working. David prayed often to be quickened, and so may we and yet be alive. It is one thing to have life, another thing to have livelihood. That may be present when this is absent; for:

1. A Christian may have a dull temper of body, not able to render unto Him the spiritual sense of spiritual duties. Melancholy intercepts the vitality not only of nature, but of grace.

2. He may not so seriously meditate and dwell upon the ways and motive of livelihood. He may have but remiss and unpiercing or unapplying thoughts of God's great love and mercy, of Christ's blood and intercession, of the promises' goodness and fullness; and, therefore, his spirit may be dull.

3. He may not have such an actual aid and special influence from the Spirit of Christ to excite his spiritual frame and temper; and then, if that wind is more slack, our ship will move on with less forwardness.

4. Or, lastly, perhaps he may have overlashed. He has been (improvidently or accidentally) in the dulling ways; he has been surfeiting upon some sin, or too greedily embracing the heavy world, or been idle in his particular calling. But whatever the cause may be, this is certain, that indisposition is not fundamental. It is not such a case which nullifies the estate of grace for, as in our most lively times, there is more duty than we can thoroughly do; in our dullest times, there is not more duty than we would do.

And this know, that the Christian condition keeps up for truth of being, notwithstanding the many pauses, the many eclipses, the many indispositions which may, and do accompany it.

But, yet again, secondly, be informed of this, that God observes the bent of the heart in the duty and, accordingly, accepts it. You know that place in the Chronicles, how that the good Lord pardoned everyone who prepared his heart to seek Him, though he was not cleansed according to the purification of the sanctuary.

The greatest actions, managed from a corrupt heart, are not accepted with God. All the superfluous and abundant gifts of the Pharisees were worthless, yet the widow's mite found acceptance. The meanest duties, set forth with a perfect heart, are acknowledged by God. He will take notice of them, for God looks to the heart. He does not eye so much your behavior; He does not listen so much to your words, but (through these) He considers your heart. If that comes with life, though your body comes with dullness, though your tongue is not so fluent, yet if there is life and truth in the heart, He will find duty and will accept it.

You remember that simile of the goldsmith who has a skillful eye to find out the smaller and neglected ways of gold, though covered with much dross; and, many times, there is much fire and much gold when both are hidden with dust and coal. So is it with the Lord. He can scent out the secrets of our desires, and what we would do is observed and taken with Him for well-done, notwithstanding the many indispositions which cover our altar. Therefore, it is David's counsel to Solomon his son, *Know thou the God of thy father, and serve Him with a perfect heart and with a willing mind, for the Lord searcheth all hearts, and understandeth all the imaginations of the thoughts. If thou seek Him, He will be found of thee, etc.*

Beloved, we are mistaken about duty. We do not judge it to be duty unless the tongue can speak much,

and our behaviors are fresh; as if a man were not a
man who did not work in coarse clothes. But we know
that the sealing of spiritual service with integrity of
heart is duty. And this is it which God considers, and
unto which He has made many promises of acceptance, audience, and grant. This is something to stay
us. Will you say, "But now we stick at this, whether the
bent of our hearts is entire, notwithstanding our indispositions and dullness"?

That may easily be discerned. You may know that
the bent of the heart is right and even in duties:

1) By not contenting yourselves with this heavy
kind of performing of duties. You will have life enough
to dislike yourselves, though you do not have power
enough to mend your services.

There are some men (and they have evil hearts)
who will be picking some help and pleas for their lazy
and dull serving of God from what has been spoken.
"O," they say, "though we cannot do as others do, yet
our hearts are as good and as willing. God knows the
heart and regards it."

He does so, and He knows this of your heart, that it
yields Him lazy service and dislikes not itself therein.
But, now, the true Christian is not satisfied with this,
that God accepts a weak heart, but it would also, hereupon, bring Him a better heart. It many times falls out
with itself and rebukes its own dullness, *Why art thou so
heavy, O my soul; and why art thou so indisposed within me?*
"You are serving a living God. Why do you not serve
Him with a more lively heart?" And then it breaks out
all of a sudden, "Well, Lord, if I had a better heart,
Thou shouldst have it; if I could find more affections, I
would bestow them on Thee." Hereupon:

2) The heart falls upon the ways of livelihood and exercises the art of quickening. It will not rest in this indisposition, but will use all the means to better itself, and this abundantly manifests its bent.

As you know, the weak person will have one turn more, and the ingenious scholar will write one line more, and the desirous archer will make one shot more. So the sincere heart will assay yet more in duty. "Perhaps frequency in duty," he says, "may breed fervency in duty." A man may get heat by walking and by rubbing his numb parts.

Or "Perhaps," he says, "one duty more in another kind, may quicken me to duty in every kind," as some medicine and cordial to the heart may cause more nimbleness in the hands and feet. "I am somewhat dull in praying. I will, therefore, read more or hear more that I may find matter to set on my prayer. I may perhaps meet with that in reading which may set me on in praying."

Or, "I am somewhat dull in hearing so I will, therefore, pray more. Perhaps God may hear my prayer, and then I may hear His Word with more attention, delight, and profit." And, assuredly so, it falls out many times that our indispositions are more about some particular duties which are singularly removed by the small dispositions, yet left in us about some other duties.

Or, "If all this does not better me, I will even go to God's ordinances, and will come before Him, and bring Him my soul thus indisposed. Perhaps yet He may be disposed to quicken me by His word, to cheer me by His sacrament. Who knows but that He may let fall a blessing, that He may so powerfully direct

Himself to me as to shake my heart, as to throw off all my dull distempers, and revive my graces, and excite my affections." So that if you perceive your dullness, if they grieve and displease you, if you will not rest in them, if you yet set out to the means of removal, assuredly your hearts are sincere.

God sees that the bent is honest, that you are indeed willing; and take this for your comfort, that if it is thus with you, God (for the present) accepts your services and, ere long, you shall be freed of these indispositions which accompany you in your services. God will drive this sleep from your eyes, and these fowls from your sacrifice. Once again, though, note that:

3) The cause of all acceptance is in Christ. Therefore, do not doubt that God will reject your services because of your indisposition, but believe He will accept your sincere endeavors because of His Christ.

Beloved, it would be good for us to consider all things about duty. A sincere heart must set it out, a gracious God must take it; and a mighty Redeemer and Intercessor must present it. Christ presents that to His Father, which we present to Christ. The duty belongs to us, but the reason of acceptation is not in the petitioner, but in the Intercessor. God accepts us not for our fullness, not for our liveliness, but for His Son's worthiness, for His merits, who ever lives to make intercession for us, who offers up the prayers of the saints with the perfume and odors of His righteousness. Are your prayers fervent? They are not accepted for their own strength. Are they weak? They are not rejected for their impotency. Is your heart sincere? Then know that Christ has a sufficiency of merits to cover your self-blamed indispositions and to gain the acceptance of the weakest (if sincere) services.

Therefore, this would be a good way, in case of disliked indispositions, not to place the acceptance in ourselves, but in Christ; and, though there are inequalities of expressions in duty in us, yet there is a constancy of intercession by Christ for us. Sometimes we come more fully, sometimes more emptily; sometimes we run, and other times all we can do is move. Sometimes affections are smart, judgments quick, expressions ready, requests fervent, hearings reverent and delightful, yet at other times the wheels are almost down, the spring moves slowly. Our affections do not turn so lively; our judgments are barren; language sticks; requests breathe only, but do not flame. We hear, give credit, stock it up, and that is all. Here you see the various carriages of our holy services in respect of the person, yet there is no such variety in Christ.

Whence it would follow that if our duties found grace with God because of their accidental vivacity in our performance, all our weaker services would be utterly lost and, in case of the more lively services, Christ also would be lost because the reason of their acceptance would be in themselves. But Christ is required to make up our duties as well as to make up our persons. He must be a Mediator for these and an Intercessor for those. And, because there is a constant merit and a perpetual offering up of that same with all the prayers of all saints, hence, it is that they are accepted not for their own worth, but for His name.

VII. A seventh spring of doubting is a conceit of successlessness in duty. We have prayed much for the perfecting of such graces, or the subduing of such corruptions, or establishing in such duties and courses, yet nothing comes of it. We are as we were, and where we were; therefore, we doubt that we are not good, or that God does not intend any good to us.

This is the spring, the cure and remedy of which may be made up by these considerations:

1. Service and progress in duty belongs to us, and their rewards and recompenses belong to God. "I have prayed a long time to God." True, and you are bound to pray still.

"I have heard a long time." True, and you are bound to hear still. You do but what you are bound to do. It is the husbandman's part to plow the land and to sow the corn; and it is God's part to give the harvest. Hereupon, says the apostle, *Let us not be weary in well-doing, for in due season we shall reap if we faint not; for God is a God hearing prayer, and He will be found of them that seek Him, and will not forsake them.*

2. God is a good Master; Job did not serve Him for nought. *I called upon the Lord, and He answered me,* said David. And, in another place, *He has heard my voice, and my supplications, and inclined His ear unto me; therefore will I call upon Him as long as I live.* Not one of the servants who trafficked with the talents could complain that He was an austere Master. Therefore, God takes it to heart when they, in Malachi, charged Him with neglect and irrecompence for serving Him. *Your words have been stout against Me, saith the Lord. How so? Ye have said it is in vain to serve God, and what profit is it that we have kept His ordinance, and that we have walked mournfully before the Lord?* Whereupon the Lord instantly manifests His bountiful and tender disposition to them who served Him, and thought on His name. *They shall be Mine* (said

He), *and when I make up My jewels, I will spare them as a man that spareth his own son.*

3. It is our duty to seek, and not only to seek, but also to wait. The Lord is a God of judgment; blessed are all of those who wait on Him. Petitioners must wait for an answer as well as present a request.

Therefore, know that faith, in point of seeking God, has a double office.

One is to deliver up in the name of Christ our wants, which God has promised to supply in His word. Another is to expect and wait those supplies which God has promised. Therefore, said David, *As the eyes of servants look unto the hand of their masters, and as the eyes of a maiden unto the hand of her mistress, so our eyes wait upon the Lord our God, until* (even so long, let it ever be so long) *that He have mercy upon us.*

And, beloved, this waiting notably distinguishes between desires which come from an unsettled humor, and those which come from poverty of spirit. In them, we give on, but presently give up, as we do in slight visits with men. We knock at the door and, if none answers, away we go. Our business was little, and so our stay is answerable; but, in those desires which spring from poverty of spirit, these have faith to believe that God is at home, and they have patience to wait His answer. As a poor beggar (suppose such a one as Lazarus) will lie at the gate and knock more than once, and wait more than an hour for some alms, for some crumbs of our tables, so will humble Christians who are truly poor in spirit. They will be at heaven's gates, put up request after request, and expect day after day the speeding of them from the throne of grace and mercy.

"But we cannot wait!"

You cannot? And that is the reason you miss your answers. If beggars will not say, they lose their alms; and, if Christians will not wait, they lose their grants.

Yet let me not go off easily from this scruple, for in it lies the choicest part of the cure. If we could but wait on God, then assuredly we would see that we have no reason to cry out of fruitlessness in seeking.

How may we learn to wait? Thus:

1) You are sure to speed. Certainty of answer will beget constancy in seeking. Sure to speed? How shall we be sure of that? Thus:

a) Take it in promises, and so you are sure.

b) Take it in performances, and so likewise you are sure; for promises, you know, have a certainty in them. We have no way to pierce God's intentions of doing us good, but by His promises; and in them we have a way. For as the words of man deliver unto us the thoughts of man, so the promises of God reveal unto us the intentions and purposes of God. Now, then, observe what God has promised to waiting, Habakkuk 2:3, *The vision is yet for an appointed time, but at the end it shall speak, and not lie; though it tarry, wait for it, because it will surely come, it will not tarry.* It is as if God had said, "Do but wait, and you shall be delivered! You shall be delivered! You shall be delivered! You shall be delivered! You shall be delivered!"

O the rhetoric of God! O the certainty of His promises!

Psalms 27:14, *Wait on the Lord: be of good courage, and He shall strengthen thy heart.* Isaiah 40:31, *They that wait upon the Lord shall renew their strength. They shall mount up with wings as eagles; they shall run and not be weary, and they shall walk and not faint.* Micah 7:7, *I will look unto the Lord, I will wait for the God of my salvation; my God will hear me.* Will you now see a certainty in performances? Then read Psalms 40:1, *I waited patiently upon the Lord, and He inclined to me, and heard my cry.* Here was waiting, and here was sure speeding. He was but one man. Then Hebrews 6:12, *Be ye followers of them who, through faith and patience, inherit the promises.* They inherited the promises, (i.e.) got all the good out of them by patient waiting. If we are sons, let us wait and then we also shall be heirs of the promises. The good of them shall be settled upon us.

See also Isaiah 25:9; and, Isaiah 49:23, *None shall be shamed who wait on me.* From all which we infer that, if God has made sure promises, if He has hitherto performed those promises unto such as wait upon Him, then, if we wait, we shall surely speed, etc.

2) The things you desire are great and worth the wait. You would think him a strange man who would not wait the sealing of the pardon which the king had promised him. It is a wonderful thing that, when God promises us pardon of sins, we cannot have patience to seek and wait the sealing of it. Yet pardon of sins is such a thing as our very life lies in it.

So, again, is not grace a singular thing? Is not mortifying of sin an excellent thing? And is it much that the Lord puts us to more frequent seekings, to repeated prayers and duties, for those gifts and grants which are so high in their nature, so admirable in their use, so saving in their end. Can you be better employed?

3) The answers will sweeten and easily recompense all the times and labors of seeking. When the

manchild is born, all the labor in travail is forgotten; the joy of it drowns the sense of that. Let God but lift up the light of His countenance on you, and it will answer and quit to all the prayers that ever you made in you life. *I found Him whom my soul loveth; I held Him,* etc.

4. Doubled services usually have doubled mercies; for, when God prepares the heart, He will incline the ear; and, when He intends a great mercy, He first enlarges the heart to a greatness of desire and seeking. Every true seeking of God opens the heart wider and secretly adds to the stock. The more prayers we have put up to use in the hands of God, the larger will the return of them prove. When we have been long suitors, God (ordinarily) at length dismisses us with more than what we ask, so that He will answer us not only for our prayers, but also for our time.

5. We shall have the best things in the fittest times; therefore, we should not accuse our services as lost, for God will answer them. But then it shall be in the best things, at the best times. "O," you will say, "is it not more than time that I had more grace, and sin more subdued?"

I answer, "Perhaps not." God knows that you have a proud temper, and you grow big and art apt to swell upon enlargements. You are apt to despise others, and to make glorious conceits of yourself and, therefore, He answers you not by victory, but by combat. That is, He does not presently subdue your sin that it shall not trouble you, but lets it alone that it shall exercise you.; You shall find matter to keep you low and humble when still you feel such remnants and workings of corruption. To the resistance of which God yet enables, and after your heart grows more emptied, you shall have victory. Again, though you pray against your sins, yet you venture upon the provocations and occasions of sin and, therefore, the Lord may justly hold up because you do not hold in. Now, the Lord, by His silence, will teach you in these times forbearance on your part as well as forbearance on His part. Then, upon your next prayers, accompanied with this watchfulness and avoiding occasions, He will let fall more strength of power to mortify your sinful dispositions.

Wherefore, let us not faint in case of suspensions, for God suspends His grants to the times when you are fitted to receive them, and when it is fit for Him to open them.

Is it sin that you would have subdued? Seek His subduing power and, withal, decline inviting occasions either from yourself or others, and then God will hear you. Now you are fitted, and now is it fit for God to help you; but, if you will pray against the disposition, and run still upon the occasion, God will not answer you.

Is it grace even in duty which you would have? Then you must use former grace and stick close with humbleness, diligence, and reverence, to the means; and now God will supply all your wants. Until you have a more humble and doing heart, you are not fitted for more grace. *God giveth more grace to the humble,* said James.

I say, He will give you more grace. You shall have enough for your condition and enough for your salvation, although you do not have such an equal measure with others, whom God intends for more public use and service than He does you.

6. God's forbearings should not occasion cessation,

but earnestness. He is not silent that we thereby should become speechless, but that our desires should grow more fervent. You know that the skillful angler does not draw back his bait that the fish should not bite, but that, by this means, he should the more greedily leap after the bait. And the tender mother steps aside, not that she would not have the child seek her, but that it may even dote after her.

So God many times draws back and steps aside; and, as the prophet Jeremiah speaks, *He becomes as a stranger, and as a wayfaring man who turneth aside,* etc. And, as David speaks, *He is as one that sleeps.* Why? What? Is it that He does not know us? No. Is it that He does not hear us? No. Is it that He will not speed us? No. Why then? Surely because:

1) He delights in this music: He smells a sweet odor and savor in all our humble sacrifices; He delights in the broken heart.

2) He loves that we should *strive with Him for His grants* (that is the phrase, Romans 15:30) and *wrestle with Him* (as Jacob) and so *prevail upon Him;* and *that we should give Him no rest,* (Isaiah 62:7), *until He has satisfied our souls with mercy, and established them with His grace.*

3) He would enhance the goodness of the things desired and make us to wear the answers with more thankfulness to Himself, with more comfort to ourselves, and with more benefit to others.

VIII. An eighth cause of doubtings is weakness of judgment about the essentials of salvation, which necessarily causes doubtings, both in respect of those suspicions, errors, and mistakings to which it is subject;

**as also in respect of that scrupulosity which ever ad-
heres to the conscience, where weakness adheres to the
judgment.**

Now the remedy of this spring consists in these particulars:

1. We are preposterous in our searches. Many a
Christian loses himself in a sea of opinions before he
has squared himself with the first grounds of religion.
Remember this, that the first truths support and maintain the rest (as the cornerstone the rest of the building) and are as the original will, which decides many
scruples in law. Hence is it, that some men doubt
about special conclusions because they are ignorant of
the general principles, which, were they distinctly
known, the falsity of any conclusion would easily become evident unto them.

Man usually disputes first and knows last. As if a
soldier would range an army before he has learned to
handle his weapons! How ordinary is it to hear disputes of original sin, of predestination, of redemption,
of faith and justification, of assurance and obedience,
of the degrees of grace and duty, of the direct and absolute way of life? I say it is ordinary to hear some arguing of these who yet are ignorant of the nature of
these. But Paul's method was to lay down his foundation of repentance from dead works and of faith towards God which, if Paul thought fit to teach, I think
fit for us to learn. That ship rolls least which is well-
founded, and that Christian doubts least who is well
grounded in the main points of religion.

Besides this, those primitive truths give an aim to
all truths, so likewise they uncase all errors, heresies,
opinions, and arguments, which come to pervert the

mind another way. And surely, when the mind obtains an evidence by one truth for another, and by truth also of error contrary unto it, it is in the least hazard of doubting; for doubtings ordinarily arise from some error or misapprehension in the mind.

2. Get a distinguishing knowledge of fundamentals from accessories. Every part of the house is not the cornerstone or the pillars. A man may take away much, and yet the house may stand. If you take away the painting and music, or some ceilings or annexed posts, yet the house may stand. So may a Christian's salvation, though he does not know many accessory truths: Nay, although he mistakes about them; nay, although he denies them, if this denial is not accompanied with a proud perverseness, but arises only from inevidence and inability.

There are three things about which it would be good for Christians to have a distinguishing knowledge: fundamentals, consequents, and indifferents.

Fundamentals. That is what I call those truths which take up the work and way of salvation: as the doctrine of sin, of Christ, faith, and repentance, etc., for these are such things without the knowledge of which no man can be saved.

Consequents. That is what I call those illations and inferences which flow from the primitive truths, either *virtute rei,* in the nature of the thing, just as a stream flows from the fountain, or *virtute intellectus,* in the judgment of the person, as the conclusion is made, by such or such a man's conjectural opinion, to flow from such a principle or such a text.

Indifferents. That is what I call those actions which, in themselves are neither holy nor evil; neither is a man by any express command from God (*specificative*) enjoined to them or (*specifically*) prohibited from them; which things considered absolutely, if a man does use them, he shall not be saved; if he does not, he shall not be damned. They no more constitute a Christian than a garment does a man; which, whether he wears it, yea or no, yet still it is a man.

Now, this distinguishing knowledge exceedingly assoils the doubting heart, which ofttimes shakes and rolls about the lawfulness of indifferents, etc.

3. Reduce all conjectures and consequent truths unto the first truth. It is the counsel of the apostle, 1 Thessalonians 5:21, *Prove all things*. And the prophet Isaiah, *To the law and to the testimony*, Isaiah 8:20.

It was a good speech of St. Augustine to Manicheus, contesting with him for audience. "Hear me, hear me," said Manicheus, "Nay," said St. Augustine, "let me not listen to you, nor you to me, but let us both listen to the Apostle, saying, *I had not known sin*, etc.

Beloved, we may see what weak creatures we are when truths fall down among us, and when we sit in the tribunal; alas, what distractions, what several stamps do our several opinions set on them! What distinctions, limitations, qualifications! We will be sure, every one of us to handle the question so that it shall be so far true as may stand with our own delights, profits, aims, and ends. We do, many times, for personal respects, discourse of and determine truths; but now reduce them to the first truths. How do our empty and contrary opinions and fancies clatter and shiver to dust! They fall down before the Word of God, as Dagon did before the ark of God; for the Scriptures are the touchstone which will easily decide counterfeit glosses and errors from genuine and proper truths. Genuine truths are like the young eagles that can, with open eyes, behold the light of the sun; and erroneous glosses and opinions are like sore eyes which cannot behold the sun without twinkling, and watering, and closing.

And note, by the way, that if the truth is the truth of God, it tends to these three things, viz. *The glory of His rich grace,* Ephesians 1:12; *settling of peace in the conscience,* Romans 5:1; and *mortifying of sin,* Titus 2:12.

4. Establish the mind in declared truths. *Beware,* said the apostle Peter, (*seeing ye know these things*) *Lest ye, being led away with the error of the wicked, fall away from your own steadfastness.*

It is not unknown, that some (like peddlers) wander up and down, and make a living by their errors; subtle people, and crafty to their own confusion, who have only a strength of parts to gloss over sins and errors and to weaken the strength of truths and ways to heaven. Most rendering children of Satan, for they cease not to pervert the right ways of the Lord; and yet, so artificially do they vent their wares, so neatly do they set them out with the applause of reason and carnal licentiousness, that many weak-headed Christians swallow up their baits, drink up their cups, lick in their tumultuous and unsettling doctrines; yea, and some of higher judgments do many times reel and stagger at the same.

What is the reason? Surely this: the master is loosing the anchor, and therefore the ship begins to toss. Men do not establish their hearts in known and approved truths; they do not confirm their faith to what God said against that bewitching discourse of reason and liberty; they will be listening to natural reason, and therefore, with Nicodemus, break out, *How can this be?* When men will not stick to truths, it is just that they should be troubled with doubts and errors. It is the apostle's counsel, 1 Thessalonians 5:21, *Hold fast that which is good.* So, 2 Timothy 1:13, *Hold fast the form of sound words,* etc. That is, clasp it; grasp it; maintain it as one would a jewel in his hands, the which another would violently force away. When the mind is rooted in truth, it will not shake with so many doubts which will assuredly spring from erroneous principles and doctrines.

5. Meddle with no more truths than will save your soul and serve your particular relation. A man may go in a shallow water, who rises and falls, waves and slips in a deeper channel. I will tell you, as all duties, so all truths do not concern all men; God does not expect or require that every Christian should be a doctor of the chair. Some points in religion are high and mysterious; others are dark, and lie yet under prediction and prophecy. But those parts which direct to your duty here, and to your salvation hereafter, are clear, express; he who runs may read them. Busy yourself most in these; study to be a good man and a good master; a good man and a good servant, etc. Exercise yourself to know what concerns you, and then to pray yourself into the practice of that. This is a wise way, and settled, and which is exempted from vain turmoils and many judicial doubtings.

6. Inform the conscience with the nature of a Christian and saving condition. Some things are required towards salvation, some things unto salvation; some things give a being, other things a comfortable

being; of all which, if a person had a special and distinct knowledge, he might walk more quietly without fears and doubtings. Shall I give you a hint of some particulars? Remember then these propositions:

1) Preparations to grace are different and unequal; all men are not prepared by the same degrees, or in the same manner, for Christ; conviction of the natural estate, and attrition, and anguish, and those legal operations, those are preparations, for men must know their sinful condition; they must have the spirit of bondage; they must be heavy and weary before they can lay hold on Christ.

Now, these legal impressions are different. Every believer (of ripe years) has felt them more or less, yet all cannot say alike. Every child feels something in his birth, but some children are brought forth with more pains, and others with less difficulty. Lydia was quickly delivered, but Paul lies by it some days. Some people can say, as David did in another case, *Sorrow endured for a night, but joy came in the morning.* Others may say, as the same David, *Night and day Thy hand was heavy upon me.* The Lord is pleased (for He is an arbitrary Agent both for the matter and manner in our spiritual alteration) to single out some persons and to charge their sins deep upon their consciences and to pursue them with singular terrors, to stick His arrows and their own sins so close that they know not which way to turn themselves. He almost grinds them to powder and casts them to the dust and to the lowest amazements and distractions; and then, as the skillful artificer, who has bruised and battered and broken the mass into pieces, and thrown it into the fire and melted it, he yet at length takes it out and fashions from all this a most comely and precious and useful vessel; so does the Lord many times with some people. He returns them their old sins, and powerfully mingles the law and their sins and their consciences together; and so with that hammer bruises and breaks their sinful hearts, and with that fire melts them, and dissolves them as it were; yet after along and sad time of sensible conviction and horrible bondage, He graciously forms the Lord Jesus in their hearts and renews His blessed image of grace, and they become the most acceptable vessels of glory; but with other persons He deals not in this high measure. He does indeed arrest them with the law, but does not so fetter and iron them; He does not so imprison them. But, upon their falling down, He is pleased to release them from their guilt and fears and to *deliver them from the powers of darkness, into the marvelous liberty of the sons of God.*

Therefore, know this, when God has attained His end, He ceases in this way of legal operation. "What is His end?" will you say. I answer, "His end is in these legal preparations":

a) To evidence unto a man the foulness of his heart and life.

b) To convince him of a total unworthiness.

c) To produce most inward dislikes of such an abominable thing as sin is.

d) To make a man willing, upon God's own conditions, to take and receive Christ. These are the ends which, in some sooner, in others later, accomplished, the Lord ceases the workings of preparation.

You know that if a piece of stone or wood will break with one or two blows, we spare the rest; and if the mass will yield in one day's firing, we then let it out. So, etc. But if yet the knottiness is great, and resistance long, then knotty wood must have iterated blows, and unyielding metal must have the greater fire. From all this, the doubtful heart may perhaps be settled about his estate in grace.

Ask him, "Do you love God?"

"I do."

"Serve Him with all your might in all your ways?"

"I do."

"Rest upon Jesus Christ?"

"I do."

"Combat and war against sin?"

"I do, and yet I fear all is not right."

"Why?"

"Because I never had such terrors as others."

Now then, inform your weak judgment if God has shown unto you your sinfulness, if He has abased you and emptied you of yourself; if sin and you are now at defiance; if you have yielded unto receiving Christ upon His terms and conditions. Though your legal preparations were not answerable to others, either for intention of strength and measure, or for extension of length and time, yet your condition is good and safe; for the humiliation which is accompanied with these issues is assuredly blessed and comfortable. If the medicine carries away the humor, though it does not make the person so sick, yet it is good. And, though a man lacks a storm to drive him to shore, yet he is safe enough if he is landed with a softer gale and tide.

2) The operations of grace are also different and unequal, notwithstanding that Christians may have one common principle and the same external means of grace. I beseech you observe this:

a) There is one and the same (specific) seed of regenerating grace in all Christians; the same spirit of holiness, of faith, of repentance, of love, etc. All Christians are bottomed alike and rooted alike for the substantial part of grace.

b) That many Christians may live under the same means of grace, as many people do live under the same light and heat of the sun, and children under the same parents.

c) That the exercises of their graces may yet be different, as children having the same school, may yet sit in several forms; and having the same food, may yet have several agilities and abilities.

So, Christians who have the same principles of believing, repenting, praying, and doing, and who have the same ministry and common assistances, may yet vary and differ in the active part of graces and duties. One may know more than another; one may rest upon God's promises more than another; one may pray with more fervency than another; one may do the other parts of duty more than another. Yet all of these may have truth of grace and may be saved.

Therefore, know that inequality of holy operation does not spring from nullity or falseness of grace, but sometimes from the variety of particular occasions, sometimes from the variety of particular ends, sometimes from the variety of particular assistance. Every Christian does not have the same forcible occasion to exercise his faith and patience.

Nor does God intend every Christian for some singular ends and services, to which He fits others by the greater improvement and use of their graces.

Neither does every man have, at all times, an equal

gale or breath of spiritual assistance to enlighten him, to excite, affect, and draw him. I might also add:

Neither does every Christian stir up the gifts and graces in him; he does not wisely, on all occasions and motions, improve his stock.

Neither does every man have the same temper and constitution, which conduces much the actions of the soul.

Neither does every calling admit unto every Christian those spaces, leisures, remissions, or vacations, which some have set on their heavenly frame and course.

It is with true Christians as it is with true men. Every man has a soul, and faculty from that soul, and action issuing out of those faculties; yet every man is not equal in the expressive ways of nature. So is it with Christians. All have truth of grace alike, but the exercise of it is different and personal.

3) As the actions of grace are different, so the degrees of grace are different. Compare one Christian with another Christian; it is as if you should compare one branch and limb of a tree with another where, though all is set in one common root, yet their particular measures are more and less. Or, it is as if one did compare the stars together where, though all are interested in the heavenly orbs, yet they differ among themselves in respect of magnitude and light. *Ye are the body of Christ* (said the apostle, 1 Corinthians 12:27) *and members in particular.* This was a glorious and gracious condition; but then, verse 29, *Are all apostles? Are all prophets? Are all teachers? Are all workers of miracles? Do all speak with tongues?* Nay, Ephesians 4:11, *He gave some apostles, and some prophets, and some evangelists, and some*

pastors and teachers.

Now, as this holds firm enough in various degrees of singular gifts for edification, so likewise it is as evident in those special graces for sanctification; for are all in the fold of Christ sheep? There are some lambs. Peter is commanded to feed both, ergo there are both. Are all in the garden of Christ cedars? There are some tender vines. Are all in the household of Christ strong men? There are some young, some babes in Christ too. So, Hebrews 5:13 and 1 John 2:12-13, *I write unto you, little children, because your sins are forgiven you, and because you have known the Father.* You see little children, though little children, though very tender Christians, yet know the Father and have pardon of sin.

Brethren, how exceedingly we disturb ourselves with doubtings here. Many people, through a weakness (I say no more) of judgment, fall out with their estate and condition, molest and afflict their hearts, close up all against themselves, suspect and foolishly reason and argue the nullity of a gracious condition, from the imperfections which they observe in their graces, from their behindments in faith and zeal, and sorrow. Ah, ignorant people who are truly industrious after the great measures of grace and will not yet quiet their fears and still their doubtings with this:

a) That such earnest pantings, inquietudes, and unsatisfiableness cannot but spring from truth of grace.

b) Then, when grace is in truth, though in the lowest measure, there the soul has interest in Christ, in all the promises, in God, in heaven, in all. Remember this, he who has least in grace does not have that which he would have. And he who has most in grace does not have that which he should have. And he who has any truth of grace has enough to change his heart and save his soul. I would believe in that fullness of assurance and reliance as you do; and, if I cannot, I will yet believe as well as I can. He who said, *O woman, great is thy faith!* said also to another, not so strong, *Thy faith has saved thee.* No man misses heaven for lack of measure, but for lack of truth. Our consolation lies much in the comparative degree, but our salvation is in the positive. Much grace will yield unto us here our heaven; and any grace, if true, will yield us heaven hereafter.

4) The separable fruits of true grace are different not only if you compare one Christian with another, but if you compare the same Christian with himself in divers times and occurrences.

a) If you compare Christian with Christian in respect of comforts, it is night with one when it is day with another; one goes on heavily oppressed, *walking in darkness* (that is the prophet's phrase, Isaiah 50:10). He does not have that sensible light of divine favor; (*Thou didst hide Thy face,* said David, *and I was troubled,* Psalms 30:7). He does not have that sensible joy or testimony of his gracious condition (*Restore unto me the joy of Thy salvation* ,Psalms 51:12). How many mourners are there in Zion, many who lament the absence of favor, of joy, of peace! Yet there are some others who believe and rejoice in believing; they see Christ in their arms, they *know whom they have believed,* and *rejoice with joy unspeakable and glorious,* 1 Peter 1:8.

b) If you compare the same Christian with himself; for it is with our days of grace as in this of nature. There are many eclipses, many variations. Job, how thankful, how patient, how confident was he. *Blessed be the name of the Lord,* and, *Should we receive good at the hand of God, and not evil?* and *Though He kill me, yet will I trust in Him.* Yet anon, how all seems to go again! He curses the day of his birth; he argues with God and expostulates much about the hardness of his condition.

So it was with David in some psalms: all in joy, all in triumph, all in peace. God deals well with him, answers him, revives him, yet presently we shall find him in his tears, in his suspicions: *Has God forgotten to be gracious?* In secret disputes with his sad soul: *Why art thou cast down, O my soul, and why art thou thus disquieted within me?* Psalm 42. Now this sensible change and contrariety in the soul no more argues the falseness of grace than the goings and comings of cheerfulness in the body conclude the lack of true life in it. The comforts of grace are an overplus of our wages which yet are held up sometimes from the most upright servant.

IX. A ninth cause of doubting is the ignorance of the doctrine of justification, for (you remember) I told you this, that sensible guilt was troublesome; a wounded condition was fearful. When a person finds just cause of fears, many sins, undeniable sins, and looks all over himself and all abroad, and can find no comforter, no one able to step in between God and his soul, no peacemaker, no one to lay his burden upon, he must necessarily be perplexed with many doubts; for the cure and remedy of which, be pleased to consider some particular propositions, which I will lay down to unfold the business and comforts of justification unto believing penitents, for to these only I address my speech:

1. In justification, our debts are charged upon

Christ. They go upon His accounts. You know that in sin there is the vicious and staining quality of it, and then there is the resulting guilt of it, which is the obligation of a sinner over to the judgment seat of God to answer for sin. Now this guilt (in which lies our debt) is charged upon Christ; therefore (said the apostle) *God was in Christ, reconciling the world to Himself, not imputing their trespasses unto them,* and has *made Him to be sin for us, who knew no sin.* You know, in law, the wife's debts are charged upon the husband and, if the debtor bis disabled, then the creditor sues the surety; *fidejussor,* or surety, and *debtor* in law, are reputed as one person. Now Christ is our *Fidejussor; He is made sin for us,* said the apostle, for us (*i.e.*) *vice nostra,* or *loco nostro,* (i.e.) in our stead, a surety for us, one who put our scores on His accounts, our burden on His shoulders; so the prophet, Isaiah 53, *He has born our griefs, and carried our sorrows.* How so? *He was wounded for our transgressions, He was bruised for our iniquities.* (i.e.) He stood in our stead. He took upon Himself the answering of our sins, the satisfying of our debts, the clearing of our guilt, and therefore was it that He was so bruised.

You remember the scapegoat, *Upon his head all the iniquities of the children of Israel, and all their transgressions in all their sins, were confessed and put, and the goat did bear upon him all their iniquities.* What is the meaning of this? Surely Jesus Christ, upon whom our sins were laid, and who alone died for the ungodly, bare our burdens away. Therefore, the believer, in the sense of guilt, should run unto Christ and offer up His blood unto the Father and say, "Lord, it is true, I owe Thee so much; yet, Father, forgive me. Remember that Thine own Son was my ransom. His blood was the price. He was my Surety and undertook to answer for my sins. I beseech Thee, accept His atonement, for He is my Surety, my redemption. Thou must be satisfied, but Christ has satisfied Thee. Not for Himself, for what sins had He of His own? But for me (gracious Father). They were my debts which He satisfied for; and look over Thy book and Thou shalt find it so, for Thou hast said, *He was made sin for us,* and that *He was wounded for our transgressions.*"

Now this is a great stay, a great comfort, that we ourselves are not to make up our accounts and reckonings, but that Christ has cleared between us and God. Therefore it is said, Ephesians 1:7, that *in His blood we have redemption, even the forgiveness of sins.*

2. In justification, the believing penitent has a universal discharge. What is that? That is, when a man is in Christ, when he is a true believer, he does not then receive a particular acquital from such or such sins, but a universal discharge from all the sins he has committed. You know the promise, Jeremiah 33:8-9, *I will pardon all their iniquities whereby they have sinned, and whereby they have transgressed against Me. And it shall be to Me a name of joy, a praise and honor.* Therefore, David, speaking of God's fullness and extent of pardoning and remitting mercy, said, Psalms 85:2, *Thou hast forgiven the iniquity of Thy people, Thou hast covered all their sins, Selah;* which covering of all sin is in sense the same with the apostle's not imputing of sin, Romans 4; 2 Corinthians 5.

This is a true axiom: Though sins are different, justification is not. When the Lord God justifies a person, the different qualities and circumstances of former sins do not hinder their pardon and discharge. You know that one may, with a pen, cross a great sum as well as a little sum, and a king can give a pardon not only for petty offenses, but also for rebellious and treasonous offenses, and so he does many times. It is, therefore, an observable passage in holy writ that there is scarcely a sin of any kind but we may read the blotting of it unto a believing and repenting person.

Original sin was the great deluge of our natures, and the first fire which enflamed the whole world of mankind, yet this sin was pardoned to Adam.

Drunkenness is another sin which the Apostle (in 1 Corinthians 6:10) raises to the height of eternal separation, yet was it pardoned to Noah, a believing penitent.

Lying is another sin which is, of itself, apt to lock the gates of heaven, Revelation 22:15, yet it was pardoned to Abraham, the father of the faithful.

Incest, that unnatural co-mixture, was yet pardoned to Lot.

Murder, a crying sin, and adultery, a fearful sin, were both pardoned unto a repenting and believing David.

Idolatry, that angering and provoking sin, a sin which unthrones God and makes the object of it a god, was yet pardoned unto Solomon.

What, should I mention more?

Impatience was a sin, yet pardoned to Job.

Passion, a sin, was yet pardoned to Jonah.

Denial of Christ against knowledge and resolution, a high sin (and such as a Donatist, upon no terms, would admit as capable of a re-acceptance), was yet graciously pardoned to Peter.

Persecuting of the gospel of Christ, blasphemy and compelling of others to blaspheme, (i.e.) injuriously and despitefully to oppose Jesus Christ, His work, His members. O how piercing and bleeding a sin! Yet it was pardoned to Paul; he obtained mercy.

Oppression and covetousness, by which a man sucks the blood and life of others, yet it was pardoned to Zaccheus.

Nay, yet once more, as you may see pardon in justification releasing all sorts of debts, so you shall find it releasing all sorts of debtors. Take one place for all, in Leviticus 4, where the Lord goes over all sorts and divisions of sinners, and appointed offerings for them all, and proclaims pardon to them all: first the priests, verse 3; then second, the whole congregation, verses 13. and 20; then third, a ruler, verses 22 and 26; then fourth, any one of the common people, verses 27, 28, and 31.

Under which four ranks He draws in all sorts and conditions of men, and not only appoints a sin offering for them all, but also accepts the same; by which, what else is meant but the power and efficacy of the blood of Christ by which all sorts of sins are pardoned to all sorts of believing and repenting sinners.

"Ah, Lord!" will many a person cry out.

"Why, what is the matter? Why are you so heavy? Why, such and such a sin heretofore."

I reply, "Is there not a justification?"

"Yes."

"And how does sin comes to be pardoned? Is it not by the blood of Christ?"

"Yes; but these were great sins."

"And did Christ die for the expiation of little sins only? What, did He satisfy for infirmities only and not for enormities also? And does Christ indeed leave the greatest debts for us to clear? Or cannot faith receive the acquital of great sins as well as indeliberate sins? Was not the sin offering for all sorts of persons? And have not all sorts of sins come within the proclamation?" No, no, my brethren, justification (without all doubt) crosses the book.

"You are a debtor," says God.

"I am, Lord," says the penitent. "I acknowledge my sins and am sorry for my transgressions, but I intend to run on the score no longer."

"You are a debtor," says God.

"I am, Lord," says the believer, "and Thou hast said, *If any man sins, he has an Advocate with the Father, Jesus Christ, the righteous, and He is the propitiation for sin;,* and I believe on Him, Lord. I take Him to be my sin offering and, in His blood only, I seek for pardon and redemption from all my sins."

This would be the way to support ourselves against our many and strong doubtings about pardon of sins. Yet the Lord knows I have repented of them, and I believe in Jesus Christ for the pardon of them. I hear and know that He is the Mediator of the New Testament and that His blood satisfies for all sorts of debtors and debts too. Though one sin may differ from another, yet His merit and satisfaction differs not from itself, but is all-sufficient. Therefore, I acknowledge the debt and rest on His blood for a full discharge.

3. Discharges in justification are not repealed; they are not called in again. Subsequent sins and falls do not nullify and evacuate former grants and pardons, for as much as:

1) Pardon of sin springs from special love and mercy, which alter not their consigned acts.

2) It is founded in an unalterable, absolute, and

constant satisfaction; for sin is not pardoned for any dignity in the person. In the person pardoned, there is no reason or cause of pardon, but that is in the blood of Christ, which blood alters, lessens, and abates not, though our carriages do.

Hence it is that pardon of sin in justification is called *the blotting out of the handwriting,* Colossians 2:14. If some writing is blurred a little, and somewhat blotted, yet it may be read. But if it is blotted out, it is no longer legible, and who can be called to account upon record when the writings are obliterated? The same phrase is used in Isaiah 44:22, *I have blotted out as a thick cloud thy transgressions, and as a cloud thy sins;* where, I think, something else falls in to our comfort, viz. that God Himself does blot out. Though an under officer should blot out an indictment, that, perhaps, may help nothing; but when the king himself does it, who is chief judge, then the indictment cannot return. Now it is the Lord Himself who blots out transgressions. He does it who alone has power of life and death, of condemning or absolving.

In like manner, there is another phrase, Micah 7:19, *Thou wilt cast all their sins into the depths of the sea.* If a thing were cast into a river which might be fathomed, then it might be brought up again; or that were cast upon the sea only, it might be discovered and taken up again; but when it is in the depths, cast into the depths, the bottom of the sea, now it cannot be fathomed up again. By which metaphor the Lord intends to express unto us the powerful energy of pardoning mercy, that our sins shall rise no more against us. He will clear them so that they (being once forgiven) shall come on the account no more; He will drown their guilt so that it shall not come up against us before Him the second time.

Therefore, Paul, discoursing about justification in Romans 4, uses another phrase to express this point, verse 7, *Blessed are they whose iniquities are forgiven, and whose sins are covered.* Covering is such an action which is opposed to disclosure and judicial evidences; and to be covered is to be hid so and closed so as not to appear with a judicial guilt upon it.

Now the Lord here is said to cover sin in justification. What is that? That is, the Lord will look on those sins no more with a judicial eye; He will not call them to account any more. That is the meaning of the phrase.

When a prince reads over many treasons, and meets with such and such which he has pardoned, he reads on. He passes by. He now takes no notice of them; he is not stirred. He sends not out against those whom he has pardoned. So it is here. This is for God to cover sin, viz. not to look on the sin pardoned with a judicial eye. It is not, as some most empty and dull heads fancy it, that God does not see sin at all, and He cannot. Of all the opinions in the world, this is the most ridiculous and childish to men who believe in an all-seeing God; but to cover sin is not simply not to see it, but to look over it as it were, and not to sit or stand upon it with a judicial eye, (i.e.) to account for pardoned sins no more.

Hence, in the New Covenant, God promising to justify or to pardon sin, He says not only *I will forgive their iniquity,* but adds, *I will remember their sin no more,* Jeremiah 31:34. What is that? That is, "If I once forgive their sin, I will not forgive it again. It shall not need again to be forgiven. Once shall serve the turn; I will remember it no more."

The meaning is, "It shall quite be forgotten. I will no more plead with them for what I have once pardoned."

I confess that the sense, fruit, and assurance of a sin pardoned may return. This may be lost and got, and the acts of faith concerning the particular pardon of a particular sin may do so; but God's justifying act, His pardoning act, is a free and constant act. Otherwise, if He pardoned us respectively upon an absolute incessation about sin, there would be no flesh living that could be justified.

4. Discharges in justification reach not only to the guilt, but also to the consequences of guilt; for it is a true rule *justificatio tollit poenalia!* Therefore, said the apostle, Romans 8:1, *There is no condemnation to them that are in Christ Jesus.* You know that if the body falls, then the shadow which attends the body that falls too. If the debt is discharged, the prison is discharged. We have, by the blood of Christ, the forgiveness of our sins and, therefore, the remission of all satisfying punishments. Why else does the apostle say, Galatians 3:13, *Christ has redeemed us from the curse of the law, being made a curse for us?* As Christ is said to be *made sin for us,* 2 Corinthians 5, so is He here said to be *made a curse for us.* He is made sin for us by taking upon Him the guilt of our sins, and He is made a curse for us by bearing that wrath and punishment which was due to us because of our sins.

Nay, let me speak a bold truth. To have sin remitted and yet to be exposed to punishment (I speak only of satisfying punishment) cannot stand with that unspotted justice of God; for no man is justly punished but by reason of unsatisfied guilt. Now, if Christ has fully and perfectly satisfied for the guilt, then punishment has no ground, unless we will say that God will punish for that which is already satisfied, or that Christ's satisfaction is not total but partial, (i.e.) He satisfied for a part and left some parts of satisfying punishment to us, which is the opinion of the papists for their human satisfactions.

But to draw up again, what a comfortable stay and support is this unto a distressed soul to see and find all in Christ: When a person, brought to the true sight and sense of sin, and loathing and forsaking of it, and to the giving of himself up into Christ, shall behold his many forepast guilts, and see these charged upon Christ, nay, and discharged by Christ, nay, and so discharged that they shall never be charged upon him again, nay, and all the consequences of guilt removed so that Christ has set him at liberty. He has made him a free man, and that against all Satan's accusations. He may hold out the blood of Christ which will answer all.

"I am a sinner, but Christ was made sin for me. I deserve damnation, but Christ was made a curse for me." If believers skilled the nature and extent and virtues of remission by the blood of Christ; if they knew and were possessed more with this part of justification, they would strengthen their faith and their comfort more, and their doubtings and fears would sink more. *Be of good comfort, thy sins are forgiven thee.*

5. One thing more which I had almost forgotten falls in, which is this, that the substantial part of justification is alike to all believers. What is that? It is this: God, for the blood of Christ, not only charges the sins

of strong believers on Christ, but of weak believers too. And these only are not discharged, but those also. True faith, in any degree, may take out all the benefits of justification; for, as justification does not admit of degrees, no more is it made over to the degrees, but to the truth of faith. So that not only Abraham, the father of the faithful, was strong in faith, but the father of the child who cried out with tears, *I believe, help mine unbelief.* He also has all the real interests, the very same real interests in the blood of Christ. You know the arm has not an interest in the head and influences thereof because it is big, or because it is strong, but because it is a member; by reason whereof the least finger and weakest member also claim and have a share. So, because every believer by true faith is made a member of Christ, he has therefore, a concurrent share in the blood of Christ, in the justification purchased by Christ. And, therefore, it is a weaker argument of weak believers to deny or doubt their discharge by Christ. "True," say they, "Christ is a strong Savior and has strong merits, and by Him is pardon of sin, and by His name a person is justified, but this is only for men of stronger faith than mine." Do not deceive nor unnecessarily afflict yourself; Christ has done great matters for great sinners, and a weak faith is a joint possessor, though no faith can be a joint purchaser of sin's remission. And thus have I briefly informed you with some notions about that part of justification which respects out sins.

There is yet another part which respects our graces and duties, from the weakness and mixture of which arise many doubtings, and such as are not to be disputed down by anything in ourselves, but only to be answered with the doctrine of justification.

"O," says the humbled sinner, and experienced in himself, "what a broken estate is here! What an imperfect draught of holiness! My very light is dim, and in all my duties there is yet undutifulness. My righteousness is defective; in my faith is much unbelief; in my prayers much coldness, irreverence, distraction. And, when I have sorrowed for my sins, I may even grieve for grieving no more, and may hate myself that I cannot otherwise hate my sins. How can I stand before God who is of purer eyes than to behold sin? Will the Lord accept such a person of such discharging of duties?"

Let me stop the complaint and close up the doubtings with a little more enlargement of the doctrine of justification. Therefore, remember:

1) Our persons stand not before God in their own righteousness, nor our own services in their own strength. Indeed, the Lord requires holiness in our natures, and holy duties from us. We are His children; we are His people. Therefore, we should be holy as our Father is holy. Therefore, the people of His pasture should serve Him. An unholy believer would be a monster upon earth. An undutiful son is a plain unbeliever; for, though Christ died for those who were once rebellious, yet He dies for none to make them licentious. So that holiness, inherent grace, is absolutely requisite to salvation. To salvation I say, but to justification in nowise. What is that? That is, though a man cannot be saved without inherent holiness, yet he is not justified by it. When he comes to account with God, he may not say this, "Lord, lo here I am. See if there is any sin in my person or defect in my holiness. I have not offended Thee. I do not need any help or any mercy. My

heart is totally clean, and my duties performed at all times in every respect for matter and manner to the full as Thou requirest. Enter into judgment with me if Thou pleasest. I will be tried by my own holiness."

2) But in the righteousness of Christ. *I desire,* said St. Paul, *to be found in Him, not having my own righteousness, which is of the law, but that which is through the faith of Christ, the righteousness which is of God by faith,* Phillipians 3:9. See more in Romans 5:19; 1 Corinthians 1:30; and 2 Corinthians 5:21.

There is such a thing as the righteousness of faith. It is none other than the righteousness of Christ. (We think little of it; we make little use of it. There is a kind of popery in us all; we look downward too much on our righteousness for justification.) And when we are to be pronounced just and righteous, when we or our services expect acceptance, it is in and by that righteousness of Jesus Christ. Whence two things arise to keep doubtings and fears off:

a) Though our holiness is weak, yet Christ's is strong. That righteousness which justifies is full. When we look upon ourselves, "Ah, Lord!" think we, "how shall we appear before God? How will He accept us? Such poor, such weak, such sinful, hollow people!"

I answer, Christ's righteousness is full. His coat was seamless; ours is made up and strangely cut, but His righteousness is complete, and *He is made unto us righteousness,* yea, that *of God,* 1 Corinthians 1:30. God has set Him out to be our righteousness, and He justifies us by it.

b) Though our services are weak, yet we are justified by Christ's righteousness. Aaron was to *bear the iniquity of the holy offerings,* Exodus 28:38. Their holy offerings had some unholy mixtures, but Aaron was to bear them; he was to take the iniquities away from them, and to make the offerings accepted.

Christ is this Aaron who, by His righteousness, covers all the blemishes, makes up all the weaknesses in holy duties. Therefore, my brethren, in all our approaches to God we should not doubt. It is the apostle's own argument, Hebrews 10:21-23, *Having such an High Priest over the house of God. Let us draw near with a true heart in full assurance of faith. Let us hold fast the profession of our faith without wavering.* It is as if the apostle had said, "If men knew what a Christ they have, what a full righteousness there is in Him, what He does with it, how He justifies their persons and justifies their services, pleads for them, beautifies them, ingratiates them with the Father, they would not doubt as much as they do. They would be better persuaded of God when they come and pray unto Him.

I remember the apostle has an excellent phrase in Hebrews 9:24, that *Christ does appear for us.* It is a metaphor from a lawyer. If a man has a case, he goes to his lawyer and reports all to him, desires him to undertake the whole business, and, upon the committing of the case to him, he appears for his plaintiff, opens the case, pleads for him before the judge, and the cause is carried. So is it with Christ. He appears for us. When a poor sinner, a weak believer, comes to Him and opens his condition, his wants, his infirmities, Christ undertakes for him. He pleads for him; He ever lives to make intercession. He moves His Father in his behalf, brings out His righteousness, His blood and merits, and what He did and suffered for him. And thus does Christ for every particular service, duty, and prayer for him who believes on Him.

X. The tenth cause of doubtings is disputation against the promises. "O," says the troubled and fearful soul, "all these promises which you produce and apply to my condition are nothing to me. They belong not to me. There is indeed goodness and truth, a wonderful worth in them, and they suit with my condition exactly, but I may not lay hold on them. I should but presume to take the bread which belongs to children, but not to dogs, not to such a sinner as I am."

Good Christians, do but track your own spirit, or the spirit of any distressed in conscience, and you shall find this to be the last hold usually of unbelief; namely, a reasoning against God's promises, the which reasoning is sometimes through mere tenderness of spirit, as when the soul has arguments to itself of that force, to represent a present incapacity of any good which God has promised, and, till they be removed, it dares not lay hold on the promises. But if they could be satisfied, then it is drawn in to believe; but sometimes there is a reasoning against the promises through willfulness of spirit, as when all the arguments of a doubting sinner are so clearly resolved and answered by the express words of God that the person cannot gainsay it. The person rather bends still against the promises than labors to honor God in them by believing. This latter reasoning is an irrational way, and unworthy of our abetting. I should think such a Christian's doubtings arise rather from a fixed heavy melancholy than any other special cause. Nevertheless, somewhat to help the other Christian, who argues and reasons against the promises merely out of tenderness and fear of his right and title, I would commend a few things to his consideration:

1. No spiritual good is furthered, nor evil weakened, by keeping the soul and God's promises asunder. Tell me seriously, is not all our help for soul and body (in the full and whole latitude of it) couched in God's promises? Are they not our wells of salvation and breasts of consolation? Our sun and shield? And what vessel has a poor sinner to draw with out of those wells? What mouth has he to milk out those breasts but faith? It is faith which knits the promises and our conditions together; it is faith which makes them to meet each other; and, till the promises meet (in their virtue and influence) with this condition of your soul, you shall never be helped or bettered by them. Till the plaster and the wound meet, it will never be a helping or healing plaster. You shall be as you were, and the promise shall be where it was; it shall never do the good till you apply it.

2. It is believing which must clear out title. "O," says the Christian, "if I knew that the promises belonged unto me, I would then believe."

I answer, first, this is a preposterous course and utterly impossible; as if there could be any well-grounded persuasion of our interest before we have any such interest. No, but personal persuasion is a consequent work; it cannot be the antecedent or leading work. You must buy the lands before you can be persuaded that they are yours.

But, second, if ever you would clear your title to the promises, you must then believe; for it is faith which entitles you and gives you interest and propriety. As the apostle spoke of a great good, *After ye believed, ye were sealed with the Holy Spirit of promise,* Ephesians 1:13, so I say in this case, if ever you would be persuaded that God seals His promises unto you, then first put your seal unto the promises. Believe, and then you shall see the good of them to be your good.

3. The ground of a Christian's believing God's promises must not be in him who is to apply them, but only in Him who makes them. O, this is it which gravels, labyrinths, and still distresses us, that we set up the grounds of faith in ourselves, and not in God! We are loth to acknowledge that the sole ground of believing is to be found only in that God promises.

It is said of Abraham, when God promised him a child in his old age, that *by faith he gave glory to God,* but how did he come so to do? The text says that *He considered not his own body, now dead,* when he was about a hundred years old, *nor the deadness of Sarah's womb*; but he considered Him who had promised, and was persuaded that what He *had promised,* He was able also to perform. Why? This is the right course to elicit or draw out our believing. We must not consider ourselves, but we must consider Him who promises. Our reasons of believing must be found in Him alone on whom we are to believe.

Therefore, I beseech you to remember that the promises of God are not only objects of faith, but they are also grounds of believing. They do not only contain excellent good for us, but likewise the motives to believe that good. Besides the goodness in them, which respectively answers our conditions, and the presenting of that goodness unto us by way of gift, there is all reason conjoined with these to affect our hearts to lay hold on them, namely:

1) A graciousness that the Lord will freely, and for His own sake, do us all that good.

2) A fidelity that the Lord, who has graciously promised, will also faithfully perform. And sufficiency of power in God to make good unto us whatsoever word of goodness is gone out of His lips. So that, from all these, a Christian, against all his doubtings, may yet see ground to believe the promises of God, because:

a) The promises are declarations of God for good unto us.

b) They are willing declarations, arising only from the good will of our God.

c) He dispenses the good in them to sinners freely, without any worthiness or desert on their parts;

d) There is not any good promised which God is not willing or able to make good.

e) Lastly, let any person believe on them, and he shall confess that faithful is that God who promised, and that God who has promised cannot lie.

But now, on the contrary, if you look for grounds of believing in and from yourselves, it cannot be that ever your hearts should be free from doubtings. If you make your own worthiness the cause of believing, you shall never come to believe. This is not to receive good from God, but to buy and purchase it, and is absolutely against the nature of free promises, as also against the disposition of true faith, which empties us of ourselves and sees the cause of all our good to be only in Him who is all goodness. Or, if you think that you must first find the good in yourselves which you are to fetch from the promises, you cannot then believe. You must unavoidably doubt still; because it is impossible for a sinner or a needy Christian ever to draw his helps out of himself, or to prevent the promises of God. As he cannot deserve any good from God promising, so he cannot bring any good to God's promises. *Ho, every one that thirsteth, come ye to the waters,* said the prophet, *and he that has no money. Come ye, buy and eat; yea, come, buy wine and milk without money and without price.* If you are a thirsty person, here is all provision freely for you.

4. Another thing which I would commend also to doubting Christians in this case shall be this: Take some solid pains to clear your entrance into covenant with God, thereby you shall clear your interest in all particular promises upon your occasions. There is a gracious covenant (spoken of in the Scripture) between God and His people. He takes us to be His people and we take Him to be our God; and, when that covenant is passed between God and a person, that there is a mutual acceptance, then the Lord estates this person into all the particular promises. As when the woman and man enter into the covenant of marriage, now all is settled on her, and she has title sufficient.

So, when the Lord God and a sinner are married to each other, when they are entered into a covenant, "Thou art my God, and none else; my heart is Thine, my life shall be Thine, etc.," the Lord says unto such a one, "And I am yours, and all My mercy is yours; My Christ is yours; My promises are yours. If you need any good for soul or body, all good is yours, I assure you."

O Christian, if this were once out of doubt, that you and God were entered into covenant, you would not so much doubt your title or question your right to apply any particular promise to any condition of exigence wherein you lie. *All are yours, and ye are Christ's, and Christ is God's,* 1 Corinthians 3:22-23.

5. Lastly, consider well whether there is nothing in Christ which may not be able to overargue your disputes against your applying the promises. I remember that Luther, in his commentary on Genesis, prescribed unto tempted persons one very compendious way to withstand all temptations whatsoever. Let Satan come anyway, or the world anyway, or sin move anyway, answer all with this only, "I am a Christian. I may not yield to any sin, for I am a Christian." And surely this also might be a compendious way to resolve the doubtings of a Christian, "I have Christ."

O Christian, if you looked more on your Christ, you might look more on the promises! When will you remember that, as there is no comfortable looking on God without Christ, there will be no confident looking on the promises of God without Christ. Christ Jesus is your Jacob's ladder; your prayers get up by Him, and God's promises come down by Him. *All the promises of God are yea and amen in Him,* 2 Corinthians 1:20.

There was a book in the Revelation which none of the elders and worthies could open, but yet the Lamb could open it. The promises are a precious book, every leaf drops myrrh and mercy, yet the weak Christian cannot open it. Nay, he is afraid to open it and read his portion there. Nevertheless, your Christ can open the promises for you; and by your Christ, as you may find a way for heaven hereafter, so you may spy a way for your comfort now.

"And why," may Christ reply to the doubting Christian, "are you afraid to believe, to believe My Father's word, and your Father's Word? Did He ever fail any who trusted on Him? Is He not willing to give who was willing to promise? Should He lose of His glory if you received of His grace? Or should you lose your comfort if you believed in His promise? Do you not care for His good? Why, then, are you troubled? Or, in good earnest, would you enjoy that good. Why, then, do you not believe? You see the worth of the commodity, but stick at the price. Did My Father ever sell grace or mercy to any upon the price of their own worthiness?

"How can you imagine Him to answer you in justice who yet deals with you upon promises; and, if worthiness must be found, tell Me, who am I? Is Christ of no worth to you, or of no worth with His Father and yours? I have died for your soul; I have reconciled your person; I have made God Himself to be yours and, therefore, His promises to be yours. If you think that God will start from His word, O you err! His promise is made with goodness, is sealed with truth, and is ratified with My blood. If you think it is an inexorable and deaf ear to your prayers, yet consider it is always an open pliable ear to My merits.

"Come, then. I once gave Myself for you, and since that I have given Myself to you. Be not afraid, O you of little faith. Look on Me, and through Me, unto God. So shall you see Him fully gracious and merciful, and holding forth the golden scepter to you. Look on Me, and through Me, unto the promises. Then shall you see them to be My purchase and your portion. Lay hold on them by faith, and enrich yourelf with them. In so doing, you shall please My Father, pleasure yourself, and honor your Savior."

XI. The eleventh spring of doubtings is the suspension of divine favor. *Thou didst hide Thy face, and I was troubled,* said David. O, the hiding of God's favor is more than the hiding of the sun, or than the withdrawments of David from Absalom! It is even the time of our fainting, the sequestration of our souls and life. *Thy favor is life,* said David again. Here now consider:

1. In these times of sequestration, a man has just cause of trouble. He should be moved at it, so that he cannot behold his God in that graciousness as before, in that lovingness, in that light of His countenance; and, verily, there is not a Christian really sensible of the divine favor who should not be as much perplexed in the clouding of it as he was affected and gladdened in the rising and discovering of it.

Beloved, it is ill with that man who can equally bear up in the absence and in the conceived presence of God's favor. Who is of that hard and unperceiving temper as not to solace his soul in finding God to be gracious; and not to be abundantly disturbed in not apprehending the wonted manifestations of His loving favor? How excessively distressed is the church in the Song of Solomon, that her beloved had withdrawn himself! And David, in the violence of his distemper and jealousy (whether culpably, I know not yet), strongly charges God (sure with much heaviness of heart) that He had forgotten to be gracious.

2. Nevertheless, in the times of such suspension, it is an error, and a dangerous error, a fruitless error, absolutely to conclude against our God, or against ourselves, of any present or hopeful interest in His blessed favor. Therefore, remember these particulars:

1) Observe the ways and times of the intercep-

tion of divine favor. This is certain, that God has ever some special end in the holding up of His countenance, and we may, and do, many times give Him just cause and reason. In the Scripture we may observe on our part ordinarily two occasions:

a) Some gross sins, which indeed are as a thick cloud to hold up the blessed light of God's countenance, for He is of purer eyes than to behold sin. These are the walls of separation; these shut the door and draw the curtains, and, like some closing discharge, fall upon the eye and indispose it to the comfortable enjoyment of the light, as we may see in David's two great sins of adultery and murder. They suspended the presence, (i.e.) the comfortable presence, of God, and held up the joy of his salvation, which he so earnestly desired to be restored, Psalm 51:11-12.

b) Remissness and carelessness in our esteems and affections towards Him in His ordinances. When Christians come to a moderation, to a cooling of their spiritual fervor, to a more negligent acquaintance with God, and a more indifferent performance of holy services and duties, then the Lord holds back, and calls in the sensible light of His countenance, as a father alters the set of his looks towards his child who is wanton upon his love and lets down the diligence of his just observance and duty.

See this in Song of Solomon 5:2, *Open to me,* (said Christ) *my sister, my love, my dove, my undefiled.* Here was a gracious entreaty, and full of wooing compellations. What does the church do now? Surely she stirs, she rises, she runs, she easily embraces these calls of Christ! No, verse 3, *I have put off my coat; how shall I put it on? I have washed my feet, how shall I defile them?* What is this? She was careless, negligent, full of excuses, so those phrases import a putting off the coat; for, as the keeping on of clothes was a sign of care and watchfulness (Nehemiah 4:23), so the putting them off was a sign of drowsiness, of a disposition prepared for sleep or rest. Nay, she had washed her feet, which was another sign of her sleepy and negligent disposition, it being the manner in those hot countries (where ordinarily they went barefooted) to wash their feet after their travel, and so prepare themselves to rest. The meaning of all which is this: she made many pretenses and delays, all which sprang from an acquired sluggishness and remissness of spirit. Now mark the issue. Though the church did not rise to open, yet Christ (verse 4) puts in His hand at the hole of the door, (i.e.) though she had neglected Him in His ministry, yet He sent into her heart a notable item of it by His spirit, and then her bowels were moved for Him. Why? What is the matter? Now *she rose,* verse 5, *and opened the door,* verse 6, *but my beloved had withdrawn himself, and was gone. I sought him but could not find him; I called him, but he gave me no answer.*

Here you see that carelessness of duty causes absence of favor. And when men are negligent in the entertainments of the means of grace, God in a just wisdom goes off with the sensible presence of His gracious favor.

2) Observe the ways of regaining God's favor suspended from us. What are those?

a) Be affected for the loss. Every absence of God's countenance should trouble us, but the loss of His favor, that should grieve us. So was it with the church there, Song of Solomon 5:4, *My bowels were moved for him,* or, my bowels sounded, rumbled, and made a troublous noise. What do these words intimate but an eminent disquiet and hearty sorrow for so great a loss, springing from so great a remissness. I say an eminent desquietude; for where bowels are mentioned, there an eminent degree is suggested, either of commiseration, as in that of God to Ephraim, Jeremiah 31:20, or of singular love and affection as of the mother to the child, or of most sorrowful affliction, as here.

Nay, so great was this sorrow and bewailment that (verse 6) her soul failed when He spoke. *My soul failed,* (i.e.) my soul went forth; it was gone; it departed because of the departure of Christ's loving favor. For, as the heart is said to go forth when men are astonished with fear, so the soul is said to go away when men are surcharged with grief and sorrow. Whence it is evident that the church was almost dead for her folly and negligence, whereby she had caused her Christ to withdraw Himself. And surely, if negligent and regardless entertainments of God, or Christ, or His Word (which cause the cessation of favor) are thus abundantly bewailed with bowels and faintings, how much more should the bowels be troubled, and the measures of grief and repentance be swelled, when the suspension of God's love and favor is caused by our injurious handling of His blessed Spirit by fighting against His motions and presuming against the directing and convincing light, to dishonor and grieve Him with the most foul iniquities.

Yet, if we can humbly and thoroughly bemoan our loss and repent of our sins, we shall behold the Lord in mercy and love again. David could not but yield out the countenance of his favor to Absalom, though an untoward son. If the clouds broke, the sun would shine again; for God will not only give, but restore, comforts to His mourners.

b) Revive your uprightness, and then God will renew His favor. *A good man* (said Solomon, Proverbs 12:2) *obtaineth favor of the Lord,* (i. e.) an upright man, a man whose heart is single, (for he is opposed to the man of many devices) whose heart is single and plain with God in his walkings, shall obtain favor from the Lord.

David assures us of it, Psalm 5:12, *Thou, Lord, wilt bless the righteous, and with favor wilt Thou compass him as with a shield.* It was a good speech of David's, Psalm 36:9, *With Thee is the fountain of life, and in Thy light shall we see light.*

Lord, Thou hast comfort and favor enough. Thy favor indeed is life, the very fountain of it, and in the light of Thy paths shall the sons of men see the light of Thy favor. For, brethren, we cannot see light by darkness; light must be seen by light; and whatsoever is contrary to light is an impediment of seeing. God's favor cannot be seen by anything which is contrary to God's nature. Crooked hearts and crooked ways, a heart and a heart, a tongue and a tongue, a life and a life, (i.e.) a doubling heart, a doubling tongue, and a doubled conversation, which has a vein of sinfulness and approbation, this the Lord hates and abhors; for God is ever single in all His dealings with men. They shall have mercy, or they shall not have it. And so He exceedingly delights in the simplicity of Christians. Let them deal ingenuously with Him, give Him all the might they have, and Him only, though they have not a present sight, yet they have a sure promise of His favor. The Lord will meet them, Isaiah 64:5, *Thou meetest Him that rejoiceth and worketh righteousness, those that remember Thee in Thy ways.* Walk towards God in uprightness, and God will walk towards you in comfort. Be a son and He will be a Father. Give Him your heart, and He will show to you His face.

Therefore, let us cast about not only for our general, but also for the services of our particular callings and relations in which, if the Lord sees us upright in walking, we shall assuredly find Him to be gracious in distributing the beams of His favor unto our souls.

3) Earnestly seek God's favor.

a) Seek it by inquiries in the ordinances of His favor. *Saw ye Him whom my soul loveth?* said the Church in her loss, Song of Solomon 3:3, unto the watchmen. And as Mary, John 20:13, weeping, *They have taken away my Lord, and I know not where they have laid Him;* And verse 15, *Sir, if thou hast born Him hence, tell me where thou hast laid Him, and I will take Him away.* What came of this? See verse 16, *Jesus saith unto her, Mary;* It was only one only word, but enough to make her turn herself and say *Rabboni.* So may it, and so does it, ofttimes fall out with us in our seekings of God's favor. The Lord meets us and shows Himself with His loving countenance in His ordinances; for these ordinances of God are the exchange, the heavenly exchange between God and His people, wherein they present unto Him their duty and He confers on them His grace and favor. So that they who have come there with sighs, *O that God would be my God!* have returned with psalms of joy, *The Lord is my God and my Father; I will praise Thee, O Lord my*

God.

b) Seek it by prayers. How abundant is David in this kind? Psalms 106:4, *Remember me, O Lord, with the favor that Thou bearest unto Thy people; O visit me with Thy salvation. 5. That I may see the good of Thy chosen.* So Psalms 4:6, *Lord, lift Thou up the light of Thy countenance upon us.* For God has promised His favor; and, therefore, His people may seek His favor. Nay, He has commanded His people to seek His favor and, therefore, they should seek it. See Psalms 27:8. *Thou saidst, Seek ye My face; My heart said unto Thee, Thy face (Lord) will I seek.* It is an unadvised folly in the suspension of God's favor to "un-son" ourselves, and "un-people" ourselves, (i.e.) to deny that grace and spiritual relation between us and God. This is not the way to gain favor; for, when we have undone our relations of children, we exclude ourselves from the expectations of favor. No, the wisest and surest way is to seek the renewing of God's loving countenance, and say as David, *Lord, Thou hast hid Thy face, and I am troubled;* yet Thou biddest me to seek Thy face, and *Thy face (Lord) will I seek* . Nay, I seek it, for *Thy favor is life;* nay, *Thy favor is better than life,* so I esteem it, so I acknowledge it, and as my life, as that which is a life unto my life, I earnestly desire it. Therefore, Lord, *Make Thy face to shine and behold me again, as Thou beholdest Thy people with Thy ancient favor. O visit me with Thy salvation, and let me see the good of Thy countenance.*

Now here take in two helpful advices more:

c) When you seek the light of God's countenance, do not blind your eyes. Remember still, that a man who will shut his eye shall hardly find. Now, nothing can see God's favor but the eye of faith, for in

Christ Jesus only we see and discern Him, our gracious God and Father. Therefore, keep open that eye. The direct workings of faith can always see God, and the reflexive will, at length, sees God to be my God. When you come unto Him thus, "Lord, I need, I prize, I desire Thy favor and countenance, and Thou hast promised it, but Thou will not keep Thy promise. Thou wilt never show the light of Thy countenance to my soul more." Now, though we seek much, no marvel we do not find the heavens to open. You must use the key as well as the hands if you will come in and see the rooms. Our hands of prayer must use the key of faith if we would open the countenance of God towards us; for faith is that which gives us our sights of God and Christ.

d) Judge not the issue by what you feel, but by what God promises. And in case, therefore, God does not show you His ancient love presently or easily, yet knock again, and provoke your heart to outbelieve all reasonings of fear and corruption. As David, Psalm 42:11, *Why art thou cast down, O my soul?, and why art thou disquieted within me? Hope thou in God, for I shall yet praise Him, who is the help of my countenance, and my God. O my God,* said he in verse 6 of that Psalm, *my soul is cast down within me!* (no question, but for the absence of God's favor). Verse 9, *My Rock, why hast Thou forgotten me? Therefore* (said he) *will I remember Thee.*

"Remember Him? O David, what encouragements do you have so to do? Your Rock seems to forget you, and all His waves and billows are gone over you. You are in a tossed and forgotten condition, and yet you say, *I will remember Thee.*"

No, see verse 8, *Yet the Lord will command His loving-*

kindness in the daytime, and in the night His song shall be with me, and my prayer unto the God of my life.

"It is true, these afflictions and sorrows are upon me, and God seems to forget me for the present, yet I will remember Him. I know He thinks on me; He has lovingkindness, and He will command it. He can show it when He pleases. I shall assuredly have it, perhaps in the daytime, perhaps in the nighttime; and, therefore, day and night will I seek Him for His lovingkindness. I will remember Him."

But how may one support himself in the interims of this suspension of divine favor? Can one be good who is thus? Or will God do good, or does He think any good of such a one? I answer, you may support yourselves thus:

By remembering the days of old, Psalms 77:7, *Will the Lord cast off forever, and will He be favorable no more?* 9. *Hath God forgotten to be gracious? This is my infirmity.* For me thus to conclude that God will not be favorable and gracious unto me because I feel Him not so, this is my weakness and sinful error; but how, then, will you support yourself? See verse 10, *I will remember the years of the right hand of the most High.* 11. *I will remember Thy wonders of old;* and, assuredly, the remembrance of what God has done is able to support us with a confident expectation of what God will yet do for us.

If we remember the days of old, the method of God's former proceedings and behavior towards us, we shall acknowledge, and so comfort ourselves that, when He withdrew, it was withdrawment either of necessity or expediency; and His loving countenance has risen again without a cloud, after a night of sorrow, after a day of seeking. For the suspensions of His favor are temporary, though His truths are eternal. *I will come again,* said Christ. And, *It was but a little* (said the church, Song of Solomon 3:4) *that I passed from them, but I found Him whom my soul loveth.*

You are in favor, though you feel none; and, though your comfort is in the feeling of it, yet your happiness is in the being of it. You are saved because God loves, not because you perceive that love, 2 Timothy 2:19, *The foundation of the Lord standeth sure; the Lord knoweth who are His.* He knows them in respect of the freeness of His election, and in respect of the immobility of His affection. He knows them still, but they know not Him still. *Is Ephraim My dear son?* Jeremiah 31:20. "He is so, but he thinks I think not so." Sometimes the walking child holds the parent, and sometimes the parent holds the child; there is safety in both respects for, while either I hold or am held, I am safe. So is it with us and God. Sometimes we lay hold on Him by faith, sometimes (nay, all times) He lays hold on us by His love. Our salvation is in this, that we are God's and God is ours; that He has our hearts and we His love, though we do not always see it.

You shall have favor, though now it is drawn up. He will behold your upright heart, and you shall see His face with joy, Isaiah 54:8, *In a little wrath I hid My face from thee for a moment, but with everlasting kindness will I have mercy on thee, saith the Lord thy Redeemer.* Therefore, the church elegantly says, Micah 7:8, *Rejoice not against me, O mine enemy: when I fall, I shall arise; when I sit in darkness, the Lord shall be a light unto me. 9. He will bring me forth to the light, and I shall behold His righteousness.* Remember this one thing: Upright and believing persons have always a favorable God, though they have not always the sense of God's favor; yea, though Satan testifies the contrary, which is the next spring of doubtings, and comes in now fitly to be handled.

XII. A twelfth spring of doubtings is the crediting of Satan's testimony about our spiritual condition and interests in God and Christ; to which, if any distressed Christian hearkens and attends, he shall never be freed from inquietudes and rowelings on mind, because Satan's testimony is ever directly or obliquely against the truth and comfort of our spiritual estate. For the remedy and cure of which spring, be pleased seriously to consider of these subsequent conclusions:

1. The final trial of our eternal estate immediately and solely appertains to the court of heaven. Indeed, the disquieting part belongs to us, but the decisive part belongs to God. We ought to search and prove ourselves, but no man has immediate power to decide his estate by acquitting or condemning himself. This must be done by the voice of God in His revealed Word which commands and forbids and, therefore, absolves or binds. No subject, you know, has this power to release or bind of himself, but that is the royal prerogative of the king. It is true, if the Word condemns us, then our consciences may do so too; and if the work absolves us, so may our consciences too. But this is *virtute prima,* not *virtute propria;* it is because the Word does it, not because conscience of itself, without the Word, can do either rightly. Whence two things arise to inform and direct us:

1) Satan's judgment of our estate is but usurped. It does not belong to him to sit upon our souls. It is against the law of nations that the same

party should be witness and judge. And we may say to him truly what the Pharisees proudly objected to Christ, *By what authority does He these things?* Or, as they to Moses, *Who made thee an judge over us?* Assuredly, the enemy of our salvation is not to be the judge of it, he being so maliciously vowed against our happiness. It is most unfit for him to decide it and, therefore, though he usurps a judgment upon Christians; yet, as David spoke in another case, *Thou, Lord, wilt not leave the righteous when he is judged.* No, assuredly, Satan shall one day be judged for taking upon him the judging of God's people. And do you think that Satan will give a true judgment unto us of our spiritual condition, who dares give in false evidence before God himself of Job, and who is said to accuse the brethren before God day and night?

2) No testimony is to be admitted which is contrary to the judgment of the Word. *Believe not every spirit,* 1 John 4:1, *but try the spirits whether they are of God.* The Word must judge us another day and, therefore, it is to judge of us now.

Satan's judgment is usurped, and our own is oftentimes erroneous, as in wicked and presumptuous sinners who sentence well for their safety, although God proclaims and pronounces bitter woes unto them. And, as our judgments are often times erroneous, so are they, in the times of distress, suspicious and hasty. We do not testify of ourselves with judgments cleared, and totally informed by the Word, of all our estate, but with judgments affected and distempered; as David in his fit, *I am cast out of Thy presence.* God did not cast him off, but his distempered judgment did cast him out.

2. Maintain the judgment of the Word against all

judgments. When a man has thoroughly viewed and pierced into the secrets of his heart and ways by the informing light of God's blessed Spirit, and takes his flesh and spirit asunder, I mean his sins, weaknesses, graces, and dispositions; and lays these, with all he knows of himself, before the Lord in a most sincere ingenuity, so that if he were now to die, he could dare venture the eternal salvation of his soul with his God, that he keeps nothing back, either of what is his own by nature, or of what is God's by grace, if now the Word decides for him that his condition is heavenly, his heart is upright, he is indeed one who is truly interested in Christ. This man or woman should now uphold this decisive testimony of the Word, lay it up as the great copy of his eternal salvation, and in case of opposite verdict and testimony, not to molest himself with reasoning and doubting, but to preserve the authority of God's testimony by believing and most upright walking with God in all the powers of duty.

There yet remain two springs of doubtings to be cured, and then I have done with that subject.

XIII. The thirteenth spring of doubtings is the new rising of old sins. This, I told you, could not but amaze the soul, to see the dead rise out of the grave again, and to read the debt as if it were not yet crossed. It exceedingly disquiets us about our spiritual condition. Now consider:

1. There are five times when we and our sins do meet:

1) One is the day of our legal humiliation, when the law, like searching medicine, enters deep, stirs up the evil humor, casts our sins into our very faces, sets

them in order before us, and reproves us for them with undeniable conviction and horror.

2) Another is the day of our piercing afflictions, when the Lord sends His messengers of wrath unto us, cuts off from us our delights, tears away our joys, crosses us in our aims, and we see God hewing our friends from us, our children from us, our earthly delights and contents; for miserable evils are oftentimes a cause to make us see our sinful evils. We many times come to perceive our faults by our punishments. Pharaoh did when the plagues were on him, *I have done evil in not letting the people go.* And Balaam, when he saw the angel and heard him threatening, *I will now return.* And so the children of Israel then saw and confessed their murmuring and stubbornness when God sent evil angels among them, (i.e.) some messengers of His wrath and displeasure.

3) A third is the time of some horrible and common judgment, whether it is upon particular persons, or a nation interested in the same guilt of sin with ourselves; for this is a time of common fire which, raging and flying up and down, makes men run unto their closets and bring out their concealed jewels. So common and extraordinary judgments return us into ourselves, and give up unto those our hidden sins which, we fear, will draw the same fire of judicial wrath upon our own persons. I do not doubt but, at the last great plague, many of the sinful botches broke out, upon a fear lest that judicial botch should have broken in upon their bodies and houses.

4) A fourth time is the time of death; for, though sin and a sinner really meet in all their course of life, yet sense of sin and a sinner do not always meet

until the day of death; for death is a strict and un-avoidable summons to give up our accounts, and then the unjust steward must look about him, how he shall answer his most just Lord and Master.

This time of meeting evidently manifests itself to our own experience; who, though we have kindled our sins in the time of our health and strength, yet have we not met with the flashes of them but in the times of sickness and weakness.

5) A last time of meeting is the Day of Judgment; and this is a most certain and infallible time. It is possible for a man to escape the legal meeting by conviction, and the miserable meeting by afflictions, judgments, and death itself (for some die like Nabal; they live wretchedly and die senselessly). But, at the Day of Judgment, they and their sins must meet, and shall; because then the secrets of all hearts shall be disclosed, and God's righteous judgment shall be evident to the hearts of all the world. Whence it is that, in this day of meeting, *they shall cry unto the mountains to fall on them, and the rocks to hide them* (but in vain) *from the wrath of Him who sits on the throne.*

2. There are several causes of the rising of sin. Some are on God's part, some on our part, some on Satan's.

1) For God's part. God many times causes our former sins to rise by the power of His mighty Spirit in the ministry of His Word. For, whereas the sinner would hush his fears, griefs, and conscience asleep, yet the Lord will not have it so. He rubs the sore, and galls the conscience, making it sensible of the guilt and wounds. He pierces, by the two-edged sword of His Word, even to the dividing asunder of soul and spirit,

and of the joints and marrow, and discerns the very thoughts and intents of the heart. He meets the person oftentimes many years after the commission of the sins, and most expressly revives and remembers them in all the acting circumstances which the sinning person either had, or would have, buried in silence and forgetfulness.

2) For our part. Thus, there is a double cause of new rising of old sins; one whereof is good, and the other is bad:

a) A new commission of the old sins, which brings back upon us the sting of the old guilt; for relapses into the disease occasion a relapse of the burden and ache. Cut your finger again and it will smart again; fall into your ague again; it will make you shake again. Relapses have ever this judgment with them, that they make a fresh wound, and the old also to bleed again. You know that in some wells there are two buckets. Put down the one and you bring up the other. So falling into the same sin again brings up the old burden again.

b) Renewed humiliations, for then we voluntarily look back upon our former accounts that, thereby, we may more humbly sue out a total discharge. Though we may sin the sin over no more, yet we may weep it over and over; and though the acting of it may be no more, yet the bewailing of it should last us forever.

3) On Satan's part, who, like an envious and malicious wretch, never gives over to throw unto us our errors and failings, though corrected with truest reformation. So Satan, who is the great cause and incentive to sin, will not cease, after our truest repentance,

to vex and sadden and (if he could) to despair our
hearts with the fresh memory of former and forsaken
sins; so that we seldom or never lay hands on a blessed
promise, or gain ourselves into the comfortable favor
of God, or delight ourselves in the sweet peace of conscience, but he fall in, and checks, and troubles us with
the representations of former sins and, perchance,
makes us let go our gracious hold, with the fears, suspicions, and chargements of former guilts.

3. Now, according to the variety of the causes fetching up upon us our former guilts, must we deliver unto
you several helps and remedies. Consider, therefore,
on God's part, there are several ends in respect of several persons, why He brings on the sins again.

1) To make the groundwork more deep and
sure. We make our tents too short for our wounds. We
sin much and defile ourselves much, and we think that
a little washing will serve the turn. O this business of
self-trial, of laying the ax to the root of the tree, of div-
ing into the secrets of sin, of applying the corrosives
unto the core and heart of our natures, goes against
us! We are quickly weary of it. Indeed, some trouble
and some bitterness we grant to be convenient; but to
be still accusing ourselves before God, still to be lash-
ing and wounding our hearts for wounding of God, ah,
this goes against us.

You shall see people sometimes very sensible of
their diseased bodies. O now some medicine would be
good! They find such aches, such distempers, surely
some medicine would be good; and some they take
which makes them excessively sick. But then away with
it, no more medicine. Yet at length, the disease comes
upon them again, and the physician prescribes more

medicine, ever that which must go to the root of the disease which, though it makes them more sick, yet it procures their safety and better health.

Beloved, God would have men (perhaps) a longer space to sit upon their sins. They stint themselves after great sins and make themselves friends with God presently. Now, the Lord knows that this skinning of the sore will spoil all, and therefore, after a short time, He returns them their sins again and deals with us as the skillful surgeon does with a man whose leg is broken and ill-set. He breaks it again that it may be well-set. So does the Lord. He breaks our souls again with the guilt of sins. He will make us know that we must bring Him more broken hearts; we shall know what it is to sin against Him and shall not make a real and lasting peace without a sound and solid humiliation. And truly, this is the great mercy of His wisdom to work thus; for hereby He makes our foundation low and sure, and hereby He prevents subsequent stirs and makes way for our surer and more comfortable apprehensions and applications of His love in Christ.

You know that a wise schoolmaster, when a boy skips from a hard lesson to that which is more easy, puts him back again and makes him say it over and over ere he takes it forth. Men think to be catching at Christ; however, they love to lay load on Him and throw their vile burdens upon Him, though perhaps they never yet weighed their vile sinnings and dishonoring of God. But the Lord will turn them back again. He will take off these pragmatic presumers and set them to learn their first lesson better. He will make them more sensible of their vile hearts, ways, and actions; they shall not so easily come off from their accursed transgressions. The Lord will hold up the comfortable answers of His favors and the sweet tastes of the Lord Jesus Christ, and make them again to sit down in bitter sorrow for piercing the Lord Christ, shedding His blood, and grieving of His Spirit; and all that men might be more humbled and more really fitted for Christ.

2) To make us more humble. I assure you oftentimes our very victories makes us proud; and that very grace, which should be a cause to abase us, occasionally and accidentally is a means to puff us. We rise too often above ourselves beyond measure. And, therefore, as to Paul, there was given a sting to abase him lest he should be overexalted. So, to many Christians, the Lord returns unto them and gives them a sensible sting of some notable guilt to abase their hearts, to put them in mind of themselves; for this reduction of former guilt gives up unto us our base and treacherous natures and the births of our own hearts.

"Ah!" says such a person, "this heart, this nature of mine, what was it? What is it if the Lord leaves it? See here the grapes, the sour grapes of this wild vine. Little reason have I to be so highly conceited of myself as long as I perceive such loathsome accounts and issues from myself."

And, verily, it makes us oftentimes to despise ourselves, to abhor ourselves in dust and ashes; and this is one great end and use which the Lord makes of former sins, to keep the heart in a very humble frame. We must have something or other still put unto us of our own which will let us see how foolish we are by nature, that is David's phrase, and how brutish we were, that is Solomon's phrase.

3) To make us more careful. The sharp remembrance of sin in a godly heart works stronger detestation and stronger watchfulness. God makes their new considerations to be our present preventions. Future commissions of sin are, many times, prevented by new impressions of former sins. "What! Should I sin thus again?" says the humble heart. "Have I not reason to crush these births? To crucify that bitter root, to pray against it, to watch against it, to resist it, to deny it which has been, and is now, a sword in my conscience?"

But, now, consider that there is a double carefulness wrought by the new rising of sin:

a) One respects the guilt of it, and here our care is to get our acquital renewed and enlarged. O how the Lord, by these risings of sin, soon causes the soul to rise up in suing out His grace and favor! It causes many a tear, many a prayer, many a wrestling with God, many pressings upon the promises, many an earnest beseeching to have our pardon and discharge more fully sealed unto our consciences by the blood of Jesus Christ and the testimony of the Spirit.

b) Another respects the sins themselves in their corrupt qualities, inclinations, and motions; and this is a greater study against them. Firmer resolutions, strengthening of covenants, confirmations of grace, of circumspection, of detestation, of resistance, of any thing or way by which the powers of sin may be more subdued and cast down.

4) To make us more thankful. Perhaps the Lord has pardoned those sins which rise anew in your heart. They do not always rise because God has not discharged their guilt, but because you have not dis-

charged your new debt. They arise as a debt for the discharge of a debt; as we used to put men in mind of their former miseries, not that thereby they are made miserable, but because thereby they should be made thankful.

Beloved, to have former sins discharged is mercy. I say mercy, yea, and a rich mercy, greater than to give a condemned person life or to give an imprisoned person liberty, far greater. There is no such mercy as that which blots out our sins, which saves a soul from hell and gives it pardon and life.

Now, great mercies should be answered with great thankfulness. You, in the sense and sting of your guilt, go with a heavy heart, with bitter sighs, with deep oppression: "O that I had mercy! O this burden! O this wound! O this sin!"

Yea, and with deep protestations, "If the Lord will but pardon it, if He will show me mercy, if He would receive me graciously, He should have the calves of my lips. I would love Him indeed; I would serve Him; I would praise and thank Him; I would speak good of His name; I would say, *Who is a God like Him, that forgiveth iniquities, transgressions and sins, and passeth by the sins of His people?*"

Well, the Lord has showed Himself like Himself, a God very gracious and merciful; but we, perhaps, have showed ourselves like ourselves, in distresses earnest, and full of promises; but in our exemptions, flat and full of forgetfulness. Now the Lord exceedingly dislikes this vanity and doubting of heart. He loves that mercy should be still acknowledged to be mercy. He would have us look back as well as to look up, and to give Him thanks for that mercy for which not long since we would have given all the world and our souls too. And, therefore, He casts unto us our accounts. He lets us thereby see what they were, and what He has done, that we may confess our error for not answering great mercy with great thankfulness.

But perhaps you will inquire, "What if we ourselves, for our part, are the cause of reviving former guilt and the sting of former sins?"

I answer, If it is by way of humiliation to seek the pardon and to make confession to the God of mercy and to get victory over them, this should no way discourage us, for this is no more hurt or prejudice to the soul than the after laying open of the wound to the surgeon to dress and cure it is prejudicial to the safety and welfare of the body. But if it is by way of commission, either by relapses into the same sins, or multiplying sin in another kind (both which will dig up again our buried and fore-past guilts), then I know no way of peace and safety, no way to allay these renewed accusations and stings, but by renewed sorrow and repentance. And, verily, what I delivered unto you heretofore about recovery from relapsing, is the course presently to be taken here.

O let us haste in before the Lord, with hearts trickling down with tears of blood for old and present wounds; the very abundance of sorrow, the bitterness of grief, the art of self-affliction! I cannot say that sorrow of sorrow, that hatred of hatred, that indignation of indignation, that revenge of revenge, that repentance of repentance, which are here necessarily required, and that too with longest continuance. Do what you will; shuffle off; cut to yourself a peace; you shall never have it. Your sins shall ever and anon gall, vex, and wound you, until you have renewed your bitterness of most humbled sorrow for renewing your filthiness and baseness of your audacious sinning.

But, then, suppose that Satan, through his malicious art, revives our former guilt by his accusations for our greater interruption and disquietude. What is now to be done?

I will show you here briefly two things: One is how you may know that the reviving of former guilt is from Satan or not. Another is what is then to be done by us.

You may know that your sins are revived by Satan from two effects. One is from the desperate issues of their reviving. You may know whether a man is a friend or a malicious enemy who revives the errors and failings among men. A friend revives them that you may be bettered either to reform, if the thing is evil, or to be circumspect whether the thing is true or false. But the malicious enemy revives them only to make you odious and loathsome. Now Satan's reviving of former sins is ever odious. It is evil for evil; his end is desperate. What is that? That is, that we might give up all possible interests in mercy, all hope of pardon and acceptance. Whence it is that, where he revives sins, former sins, he bends the heart to some present mischief to renounce all hope of mercy, and to self-murder, and such desperate issues; both which are against the ends of God and the desires of a holy heart; which, upon their reviving of sin, ever propose mercy and betterment unto the soul.

Another is from the filthy issues, which is this: he revives the sting of sin that he may make us more bold and mad in sinning. He revives sin unto sin; there is no hope of mercy, of recovery; therefore, it is as good to go on as not. Whence he inclines the heart to a leaping into the water, to a wallowing in the mire, to a greediness in the course of sinning, which he more easily wins from the evil hearts of evil men by those temporary allayments and cessations of stinging guilt, which they observe in themselves by their furious, constant, and hardening revolutions of exercise or the same sins.

So that, if you whose hearts are tender have been humbled for former sins, and are so upright as still to hate them, if former guilts are revived with an inclination either to give up all mercy or to give over yourselves now with licentiousness to the same or other sins; here is Satan in this: Satan now revives your guilt, and now another course is to be taken.

The course, then, is this, and I beseech you mark it:

1. Strengthen your heart with more detestations of the sins. The more he revives the guilty accusation, the more you must revive your upright detestations. And, as he pours out malice to disturb your conscience, so must you pour out revenge to subdue the grounds of it. And if he vexes you, go and vex your sins.

2. Believe not a malicious accuser. Satan oftentimes serves a writ in the king's name without the king's seal. He forgives where God does not, and he binds where God has released; and know this, *It is God that justifieth. Who then shall condemn?* If the king himself has pardoned you, how unjust is it for the under-officer to arrest and challenge?

3. But in case of frequent inquietudes, when Satan will not be answered, but still charges, now make your appeal from him to God; and if he charges you in the court of conscience, remove it wisely to the higher

court of heaven. Let God once more have the hearing and the deciding.

"And now Satan, what have you to say unto me?"

"You have sinned," says Satan, "and your Judge knows the truth of this indictment."

"I have, Satan. I confess it, and my God knows the truth of my sorrow and repentance. Lord, dost Thou not know my tears, my returnings, my judgings of myself, my feeling of mercy and grace? Lord, Thou hast known it and hast known my soul with Thy pardoning and accepting mercy."

4. Rest the soul and fasten it unto the blood of Christ, which will always cry down the testimonies and clamors of guilt. Nothing but that will satisfy God and vanquish Satan; and then, by faith, not only lay hand on mercy, but hold out the stability of mercy. The king's pardon will serve twenty years hence in case of suit. Satan may often trouble and question, but God's accepting of you into mercy will (I am sure it may) quiet and uphold you.

XIV. The last spring of doubtings is silence in the conscience, long silence there.

For the closing of this spring, this subject of doubtings, observe these particulars in a word: (1) The speech of conscience, what that is; (2) The speechlessness of conscience, what and how; (3) To make conscience speak again, what is required; (4) To support ourselves in the times of its silence, what can and may do so.

1. The speech of conscience. This is more than its testimony for us or against us; for conscience is intimate with our secret frames, intentions, motives, and

actions. By its natural light, it can tell much, by implanted light more, by renewed and sanctified light most of all. Now the speech of conscience for us is nothing else but an approbation of our estate, answerable to the Word, acquitting us against all fears and objections that we are the sons of God, that we are truly changed, that we sincerely love Him, believe in Christ, and walk before Him; for really the voice of conscience is but the echo of the voice of the Word, and says that unto us touching our particular, that the Word delivers in the general. Its voice is but the assumption, and the voice of the Word is but the proposition. The Word says, "that should be"; and conscience says, "Here it is." The Word requires such and such things in a man to be saved, and who is in favor with God, and conscience brings them out and answers for the person.

2. The speechlessness or silence of conscience is the suspension of its determining and acquitting acts touching our estate in general, or touching some particular doubts. Sometimes conscience calls upon us, and sometimes we call upon conscience. In matters of direction to practice or forbearance, we usually hear a real and inward word, "Do it not," or, "You may do it." In after-doubts, we call upon conscience for its testimony: "In the uprightness of my heart I did it, and my conscience bears me witness."

Now, of all the silences of conscience, that is heaviest which befalls us in our spiritual combats and trials; wherein our gracious condition is questioned, but cannot be issued because conscience holds up and does not testify for us by any sensible approbation and acquittance, which is caused diversly:

1) Sometimes through particular misbehaviors

against the directing voice of conscience, these hold in the acquitting voice of conscience; for conscience will not speak for us if we presume to sin against it.

2) Sometimes through disregard to the voice of God in the ministry; for conscience does not take that well which the Word takes ill. And, therefore, God usually makes us know our neglects of His Word by the silences of our consciences. And, assuredly, something is ordinarily amiss when conscience speaks unto us neither good nor bad.

3) Sometimes conscience is silent to make us look higher than conscience, and that we might know there is a higher Court to which we must make our addresses.

4) Sometimes conscience is silent to makes us see upon what bottoms our faith is grounded, whether we can believe because God says, as well as rejoice because conscience speaks.

3. But to make conscience speak, what must we do? We have had its gracious testimonies by which we have been much comforted and supported. How shall we recover it to speech again? I answer:

1) Speak to God, and then God may speak to conscience, and conscience will speak to you. God has a greater command over conscience than it has over us. It is with God and conscience as with a king and his courtiers. Let the king speak kindly to a petitioner, and the courtiers will then embrace him lovingly; and indeed conscience will carry God's face and express His dispositions of love. Therefore, do this, speak to the Lord:

a) To show you the cause of conscience's silence.

b) To give the testimony of His own Spirit, which will draw with it again the testimony of your own conscience, Romans 8:16.

2) Speak to duty; be sure you do not displease conscience. If you have, repent and add no more to make conscience displeased or silent.

4. But how may we support ourselves in the times of silence? I answer, you may comfort yourself if,

1) The Word can approve you. The testimony of the Word is ever open, though that of conscience is not. What is the reason? Because men may have a constant audience and trial of their estates. And take one thing by the way; if the Word, which is always open and speaking, acquits you, conscience (though now silent, whensoever it speaks) will clear you.

2) You have, and do, approve the Word. How is that? That is, if the Word is your rule, your light, by which you have and do walk; for when conscience comes to speak, it gives its sentence from the Word (by which you walk), and of your frame and course, which you preserve in an upright answerableness to the directions of the Word.

An Addition of Four Causes of Doubtings, With a Brief Resolution of Them

I. Sense of sinful workings. "O!" says a distressed soul, "certainly my condition is stark, and I have no right to Christ, nor to any mercy. I may not believe. Why? Because I never found such vile workings of heart as of late. I feel wonderful rebellion in my heart; I cannot think on any good, nor set upon any good, but an army of evil is in me, opposing and hindering me.

To a soul in such a condition, I would (for his help) prescribe these five subsequent considerations:

1. When grace comes in truth, it is ever of that power to make such discoveries, and to raise such stirs, as the soul never felt before; for grace is a new nature, a new light, and a new active principle. It is put into the soul for that very end, to find and lay out sin; yea, and to expel and thrust it out. The judgment was never so convinced before, nor conscience so qualified before, nor the will and affections so spiritualized before; therefore, never marvel at the strange workings. When a child is conceived in the womb, it is not now with the woman as in former times; and, whenever Christ is formed in the soul, it is not with that soul as in old times. There is that now fallen, in which must purge

you and rule you.

2. If good is wrought, evil will work and oppose it. When Christ was born, all Jerusalem was troubled; so, when grace is wrought, sin will stir. Indeed, if grace came into the soul, either by a final and total cessation of sin, so that there was no sin residing in the soul, into the which grace comes, then you would feel no stir at all. Thus it shall be in heaven. Grace there shall be alone; holiness, and nothing but holiness there, and therefore, no combat, no stir. But this it never will be on earth. Sin may be alone in some men's hearts, but grace is never alone in any man's heart in this life; or, if grace came into the soul by a peaceable resignation, if sinful flesh would, without any more ado, make a full and free surrender, and give it possession without any dispute and cavil, then also you might expect a calmness, and a cessation of arms, no vile stirrings. But O, Christian, grace and sin, *The spirit and the flesh are contrary one to the other*, and therefore, they lust one against the other. Fire and water will not lie quiet. Sad, indeed, would your condition be if you had such a frame of (vain) good, against which no sinful part in you would oppose.

Every regenerate man has a double man in him: the new man and the old man. That would do good, this would not do good; that would pray; this would not; that would mourn, this would not; that would believe; this would not.

3. But then, third, you who feel such a rebelling and opposing flesh in you, what is it which you oppose? It is true, you feel an untoward rebellious nature yet within you, but what side do you take? *It is not I*, said Paul, *but sin that dwelleth in me*. Sin in him opposed

good, but Paul himself approved good, and delighted in good, and willed good.

The same apostle, speaking of the cohabitation, and the cooperation of flesh and spirit in regenerate persons, that the one lusted against the other, and the one was contrary to the other, and that by reason of the rebellion and unruliness of the one, *we could not do the good which we would;* he yet comforts them in such a condition in the next words: *If ye be led by the Spirit, ye are not under the law;* as if he had said, "Notwithstanding all this rebellious opposition of your flesh, if yet you yield not to be servants to it, but approve of, and incline unto, and follow in your hearts and courses the rules of the Spirit, the condition is very good and safe." So that, though the evil remaining in us opposes the good in us, yet, if we ourselves oppose not the good, our condition may be good.

4. Fourth, as there is evil in opposing you in any good, so there is something in you also opposing that evil. Do you not condemn that hardness which hinders you from mourning, and shed many tears because you cannot mourn? Do you not strive with the Lord by many prayers, and in the use of all His ordinances, against that unbelieving and rebelliously working nature of yours? Do you not, with Paul, conflict with it, groan under it, cry out, *O wretched man that I am, who shall deliver me?* And surely neither the sense of this, nor the resistance of this, nor the second desires of deliverance from this, can be any evil signs of your condition.

5. Last, in the sense of inward rebellions and workings, your way is not to nourish doubting, but your duty it is to stir up believing. When Paul felt that agony

between the law of his members and the law of his mind, indeed he was much troubled at it, yet he did not conclude against his condition in grace. No, he acquited that (Romans 7:25, *So then with the mind I myself serve the law of God, though with the flesh the law of sin*) and sets his faith to work, verse 24, *Who shall deliver me?* Verse 25, *I thank God through Jesus Christ our Lord.* Mark his practice: "This is my condition. I feel rebellious lusts; yea, I feel them sometimes captivating me. What course shall I now take to be delivered of them, to vanquish them? I conflict with them, but I cannot conquer them. I cannot conquer them, yea, but Jesus Christ can conquer them and deliver me from them, and to Him will I go by faith."

Thus must you do in the sense of that native rebellion and vile operation of your flesh. You must by faith go unto Christ; you must acknowledge your vileness and your insufficiency, and also His sufficiency. You must exalt Jesus Christ by faith in His mediatorship and trust on Him that He will, by His Almighty Spirit, crucify your sinful flesh more, and (which was one end of His coming into the world) destroy those works of sin and Satan.

II. Another cause of doubting in a Christian may be the sense of wrath. "O!" says such a one, "would you have me to believe, or do you imagine, that I can do so and so, I who feel the very wrath of God in my soul and the terrors of the Almighty wounding me for my transgressions? What? Can or may I believe mercy for me, who now feels wrath upon me? Can I believe that God will be merciful, whom I sensibly apprehend to be wrathful?"

This is a notable case and needs a wary and circumspect resolution; nevertheless, I shall at least endeavor to ungird this burden for a troubled soul.

1. There are two sorts of persons who, in this life, may feel the wrath of God:

First, such as are unquestionably wicked, of whom some of them feel the wrath of God as the beginning of their everlasting perdition. That wrath inflicted on them is but the beginning of a just hell due unto them. Thus Judas felt the wrath of God. And some of them feel the wrath of God as a means for their humiliation and conversion. Thus, they in Acts 2:37 who were *pricked in their hearts* and thereupon cried out, *What shall we do?* felt the wrath of God.

Second, such as are unquestionably good, of whom some have felt God's wrath in case of desertion, as Heman, Ezra, Job, and others; and some in case of notorious corruption or sinning, as David, whose bones were broken for it, and God's face hidden from him for it, and his *moisture turned into the drought of summer.*

2. Again, you must distinguish those effects which appear in persons under the sense of divine wrath, for they are two-fold:

1) Some feel the wrath of God and are withal only enraged against God with blasphemies, or enraging their hearts the more to go on in sinning against God, thinking at least by the pleasure of sin to drown the sense of wrath; or running into absolute despair of God's mercy, and, therefore, never attempting any course of repentance, because they give up all hope of mercy. Where there is such a sense of wrath as this, in all respects, and forever, the condition is very fearful.

2) Some feel the wrath of God and are, here-

upon (occasionally), induced either to the study and care of a holy reformation of their sinful hearts and ways, or to a particular restoration of themselves from gross sins into which they are fallen, and for which now they feel the sore displeasures of an angry Father.

If your condition is either of these, that you feel wrath, and that has driven you to a search of your natural estate, and to the discovery of it, and to a humbling for it, and to all the means by which you may be delivered as well (and rather) from your sinfulness as from God's wrath; or if this wrath felt awakens your conscience and has been a means to scourge you out of some particular sinning, to your former and better walkings with God, you may now safely believe on mercy. Yea, though you as yet feel wrath, yet you may believe mercy. And my reason is this: now mercy is your portion; your condition now is right under many promises of mercy to pardon you, for it is a truly penitential condition. See Isaiah 55:7; Ezekiel 18:21-22; and Hosea 14:1,2,4.

3) Though mercy is your portion, yet know that the sense of wrath will not be off until you believe actually on that mercy. It is not mercy in the promise which alone can remove the sense of wrath, but it must be mercy applied by faith; for till faith works in the soul of a man, till the poor soul looks on God through the perspective of faith, God does not appear as a merciful God, but as a wrathful God. And, therefore, you being in such a condition as I have delivered, you may safely venture on mercy, though you feel wrath (the forenamed saints did so); and, upon believing, you shall in due time feel the sense of mercy to take off the sense of wrath. Your faith will see a reconciled God,

and then you shall enjoy a pacified conscience.

III. A third cause of doubting may be a condemning conscience. "But," says the trembling Christian, "my conscience tells me of my sinnings and of wonderful sinfulness within me; and God is greater than my conscience, who will assuredly condemn me. O, I may not believe!" This seems to be a knotty case, whether a person may believe God's absolving him, though conscience in him is condemning. I will deliver my opinion thus:

1. First, you must distinguish a condemning conscience. Conscience may either condemn: a man's actions or his person.

1) A man's actions are condemned by conscience when conscience, being rightly enlightened and informed by the Word of God, pronounces that they are evil and damnable; that they are contrary to God's holiness and glory and, therefore, are to be abhorred, crucified, and forsaken.

2) A man's person is condemned by conscience not only when conscience finds sin in the person, but likewise the person in sins; (i.e.) not only such corruptions in the heart, but also the heart approving, loving them, and resolved to keep and go on in them.

Now observe me in two conclusions answerable to these two propositions: If conscience condemns your person, I confess you have no reason to believe mercy for yourself. If your conscience tells you to the face of God, "You are in a foul, sinful course and have been called upon by the voice of the Word, and its voice to come out of it, and you do not leave it. Nay, you are resolved to pursue it and to insist on it!" Now, God is greater than your conscience and will assuredly condemn you.

If conscience condemns your actions only, then you may, notwithstanding that condemnation, believe on mercy. My meaning is this: though the conscience, by its discerning light, represents unto you much sinfulness in your nature and former course, and though it condemns these to be vile and most fit to be crucified, abhorred, and forsaken, this condemnation hinders not the right of believing. Nay, no man indeed should believe unless his conscience condemns sin in him; not only shows him his sins, but assures him that they are evil and unworthy of his love; nay, most worthy of his detestation and mortification.

2. Second, you must distinguish times when conscience condemns a man. There are two times of a Christian:

1) Some are open and free. He is himself and, beside that, he hears both parties; what is for himself as well as what is against himself. Yea, and he weighs matters in controversy in the right balance of God's sanctuary, not in Satan's balance of cunning suggestions. Will conscience condemn your person at such a time and under such circumstances? Nay, will not the Word of God acquit you at such a time against all fears for the substance and reality of pious condition?

2) Some are clouded and darkened, either with melancholy or afflictions, or temptations wherein the Christian sees his face through a false glass (just as a title is made by a deceitful and cunning lawyer), not according to truth; not all of it, but some of it. What is past heretofore for action and affection, or what has fallen out, not in the course of life since a man's

conversion, but only in case of surprisal and captivity. Now, perhaps conscience may condemn you, but this is an illegal sentence; it is a corrupted judgment and is reversible. God will not judge you, as conscience, in such a case, does; nay, He will repeal and disanull it.

IV. A fourth cause of doubtings is a fear lest a man has sinned that great sin against the Holy Ghost; and the main inducement to credit this is a sinning against clear knowledge, which is one ingredient in that sin. "Now this is my condition," says a troubled soul, "I have not only sinned, but also sinned against light shining in the ministry, and working on my conscience; therefore, I may rather conclude than question it; mercy does not belongs to me."

To help a conscience thus enthralled, I would wish that such a person would be informed or be directed. The information which I would commend in this case, is four-fold:

1. First, that the sin against the Holy Ghost is not any sin which a man commits through ignorance, whatever the sin or sins have been (whereof the party stands guilty), whether against the law or against the gospel. Suppose it is one of many heinous sins, yet, if the person is in a state of blindness and ignorance, if there is a nescience of the fact, if he knows not what he does, this ignorance privileges the sinnings thus far, that, therefore, they are not the sin against the Holy Ghost.

2. Second, the sin against the Holy Ghost is not any sin against the gospel which is elicited and acted through a misbelief or mispersuasion. If the sin is a slighting of evangelical doctrines, nay, a persecuting of

them, and of the professors of them, yet, if these acts of opposition depend totally on error in judgment, on a judgment mispersuaded, (i.e.) rather believing them not to be truths, rather thinking those ways to be false ways; I say this misbelief preserves such sinnings yet from being sins against the Holy Ghost because the sin against the Holy Ghost supposes light even to conviction and approbation. See Hebrews 6:4-5.

3. Third, the sin against the Holy Ghost is not every sinning against knowledge. These are not reciprocal propositions: Every sin against the Holy Ghost is sin against knowledge, and every sin against knowledge is the sin against the Holy Ghost. The former is true, but the latter is not; for many a converted man sins against knowledge, who yet never sinned the sin against the Holy Ghost.

In two cases, a man sinning against knowledge does not yet sin that sin against the Holy Ghost. One is the case of a strong and violent temptation. Another is the case of a sudden and turbulent passion. It is the same with Peter's case against his knowledge, denying and forswearing his Master. If Paul, before his conversion, had had Peter's knowledge, he would have sinned this sin against the Holy Ghost; and, if Peter, in his denial, had had Paul's malice joined with his knowledge, he would also have sinned that sin; but the misbelief of the one before his conversion, and the infirmity of the other after it, preserved them from this sin. Error misled the one, and sudden fear surprised the other.

4. Fourth, there are three horrible sinnings which attend that sin against the Holy Ghost; and the Scripture (which we were best exceeding wary to follow in resolving this case) expressly delivers them:

1) One is total apostasy from the truths of Jesus Christ known and tasted. The truths of Christ must:

a) Be known and apprehended.

b) Be known and tasted; they must be approved.

c) And then the person falls from these.

d) Nay, his fall is not particular (which is incident to the best). It is a total fall, not a falling in the way, but a falling from the way of truth, Hebrews 6:4, *If they were once enlightened and tasted*, etc. *If*, verse 6, *they shall fall away*.

2) A second is a malicious oppugnation of that truth which was once known and tasted, and from which now the person is fallen, called in Hebrews 6:6, *a crucifying of the Son of God afresh;* and Hebrews 10:26, *a willful sinning after that we have received the knowledge of the truth*. And it was evident in the Pharisees who saw and knew the light but hated and persecuted it unto the death.

3) A third is final impenitence. Whoever sins the sin against the Holy Ghost neither repents nor can repent. He is so justly and forever forsaken of God, and given up to a reprobate sense and a seared conscience, that he cannot repent. Though (perhaps) he may see his course to be evil, yet it is impossible (said the apostle in Hebrews 6:6) to renew him to repentance.

FINIS

APPENDIX

The Nature and Danger of Heresies

Opened in a Sermon before the Honorable House of
Commons, January 27, 1646 at Margaret's,
Westminster, being the day of their
Solemn Monthly Fast

by Obadiah Sedgwick, B.D.
Minister of God's Word at Covent-Garden

*But there were false prophets also among the people, even as
there shall be false teachers among you, who privily shall bring
in damnable heresies, even denying the Lord that bought
them, and bring upon themselves swift destruction.*

(2 Peter 2:1)

*Ye therefore, beloved, seeing ye know these things before, beware
lest ye also, being led away with the error of the wicked, fall
from your own steadfastness; but grow in grace and in the
knowledge of our Lord and Savior, Jesus Christ.*

(2 Peter 3:17-18)

First published in London
Printed by M.F. for Samuel Gellibrand
at the Brazen Serpent in Paul's Churchyard
1647

To The Honorable
House of Commons,
Now Assembled in Parliament:

Having received your commands to preach that which first presented itself unto my thoughts was the subject of this ensuing discourse, a theme (if I understand the present posture of these times) both seasonable and necessary. There are some points of difference which are of an inferior consequence, and stand further off from the foundation, these being but *Judicia domestica*. I do not meddle with these, but there are other positions which pull hard at the very foundation, and which subvert the faith. Against these I hold it my duty as a Christian, as a minister of Christ, and as your servant, to declare it myself. And I beseech you, before whom was it more fit to open those ulcerous sores than before yourselves (Right Honorable) who, under God, are our most choice and tender physicians?

If any reader should now be so unhappy in his charity as to calumniate this discovery of heresies and blasphemies to be an arrow subtlely designed against holiness and good men, to such a one all that I would reply is this: 1) The surest friends to holiness have been the sharpest enemies to errors; Christ and His apostles were so; 2) That I never yet have learned what direct advantage at any time redounded to true sanctity by a patient endurance of heresy and blasphemy; 3) Nor can I be so uncharitable as to think that

that any person sincerely holy, or intending the progress of holiness, dares to be a friend to such damnable and soul-destroying errors. The design which I would commend to all in this time of reformation is this: that truth and holiness (which are so naturally combined and so mutually interested) may be conscientiously promoted with equal zeal. Encourage holiness, but contend for the truth too. Maintain the truth, but countenance holiness too.

He who pretends holiness but regards not truth, and he who pretends the truth but regards not holiness, neither of these is a cordial friend either to truth or holiness. Right Honorable, be pleased to go on (as you have begun) in the strenuous support of them both. Both of them have a necessary respect to God's glory. Both of them have a necessary respect to man's salvation. Both of them have a necessary respect to our present reformation. Both of them will prove the kingdom's safety, your conscience's comfort, and the crown of all your long and great labors. For both of these, you have the prayers of

> Your most unworthy,
> yet most faithful servant,
>
> *Obadiah Sedgwick*

The Nature and Danger of Heresies

And the serpent cast out of his mouth water as a flood after the woman, that he might cause her to be carried away of the flood. And the earth helped the woman, and the earth opened her mouth, and swallowed up the flood which the dragon cast out of his mouth.   Revelation 12:15-16

This text is a seasonable text, seasonable to the times wherein we live and seasonable to the work of this day, which should be humbling work and reforming work. The parts of the text are two: a renewed danger, verse 15, and a renewed succour, verse 16.

I. The new danger is set forth in four particulars:

1. By the author of it [*and the serpent*]. There is a former danger mentioned in verses 12-13. That was managed by the wrathful dragon; and here is a new danger, which is contrived by the cunning serpent. Open cruelty is more dreadful, but subtle policy is more pernicious. The cunning devil is a more mischievous enemy to the Church of Christ than the raging devil. Nero and Diocletian were sore enemies to the Church, but of all the Emperor Julian is reputed the worst.

2. By the engine of it [*the serpent cast out of his mouth*]. It is a question among the schoolmen whether *peccata oris* may not be worse than *peccata operis*. I am sure that the danger which comes out of the mouth of the serpent far exceeds that danger which depends

upon the sword of the dragon.

There is a mouth of truth, and that is God's mouth. There is a mouth of peace, and that is Christ's mouth. There is a mouth of prayer, and that is a good man's mouth. There is a mouth of cursing, and that is the wicked man's mouth. There is a mouth of mischief, and that is the serpent's mouth. When the devil wrecked Adam and Eve, he used the mouth of the serpent; and when he deceived Ahab, he became a lying spirit in the mouth of the false prophets. When he would deceive the whole world, he falls into the mouth of the beast to speak great things. And here, intending to destroy the Church, he uses the mouth of the serpent.

3. By the matter of it [*and the serpent cast out of his mouth water as a flood*]. It is not said that he cast out water only (and yet even that dropping out of the mouth of a serpent has been sufficiently dangerous), but he cast out water as a flood. Floods in Scripture are the paraphrases of the most extreme dangers. When the danger is sudden, high, violent, and quick, then it is expressed by the metaphor of a flood. Davids speaks of *floods of ungodly men* in Psalm 18:4. The prophet speaks of the *enemy coming in like a flood,* Isaiah 59:19.

4. By the scope or intention of it [*that he might cause the woman to be carried away of the flood*]. There was a flood which bore up the ark, but here is a flood to overwhelm and drown the ark. Whichever way the devil and his angels attempt against the Church of Christ, no less than the utter ruin of it is still the aim and project. When the devil rages like a dragon, his intent is utterly to waste; and, when he acts as a serpent, then his design is utterly to sink the Church.

II. Thus you see the Church's new danger; but now behold the Church's renewed succour. And, indeed, it is very remarkable that this chapter is as full of succours as it is of dangers. In verse 7, you may read of the *dragon and his angels appearing in the field and fighting,* but then you read of *Michael and his angels succouring even to victory* in verses 8-9. Again, in verse 13, you find the dragon *persecuting the woman which brought forth the man child,* but then also you read that there was given to the woman *two great wings of a great eagle, that she might fly into the wilderness,* verse 14. And here you see a flood cast out to carry away the woman, but withal you read of a gracious and present succour: *And the earth helped the woman by opening her mouth, and swallowing up the flood which the dragon cast out of his mouth.*

Thus you have the distribution of the text. Now I proceed to the propositions which may be observed from it. The whole state and sum of this text may be resolved into these three conclusions:

1. That the mischief which Satan cannot compass by open cruelty he will assay against the Church of Christ by subtle policy. When he fails as a dragon, then he will try what he can do as a serpent.

2. That the serpent's flood is the chief and worst of the Church's dangers.

3. That the Lord still has raised fresh succours for the Church against the fresh dangers of the Church.

Concerning the first of these, I intend to have demonstrated both the truth of it and the practice of it in all ages of the Church, as well as the several methods, wiles, stratagems, and designs of Satan upon and against the Church of Christ, and the reasons of shifting his hand and making use of his mouth, of desisting from open cruelty and falling to his wiles of policy. And then, also, I intend to show the wonderful mischief that has redounded thereby that, whereas his cruelty has killed thousands, his policy has slain ten thousands, where also might have been revealed: (1) The advantages of policy above cruelty; (2) The general receptivity or capacity in men to be taught by the policies of this serpent; (3) The usual inadvertencies rather under the workings of the serpent than of the devil; and (4) The specious ways of insinuating his mischief in the ways of policy.

But I was taken off from my purpose in the handling of this point (though, as to my own opinion, very necessary and excellent) because I should thereby check myself in the handling of the second point, which I desired chiefly to discourse upon this day before this Honorable Audience. And, therefore, omitting other things, I address myself unto that proposition which shall be the only subject of my present pains. The proposition is this: The serpent's flood is the chief and worst of the Church's dangers [*The serpent cast out of his mouth a flood to carry away the woman*].

Interpeters are carried away with several conjectures concerning this flood which is cast out to carry away the Church. There is a flood of tears and a flood of reproaches and slanders. That is a flood wherein we should drown our sins; this is a flood wherein men drown our names. And there is a flood of persecution, and a flood of invasion, and a flood of erroneous opinions, which, of these three latter it is, may be questioned.

Some, by this flood of waters, understand the flood of blood let out by the pagan emperors. A red sea was that cloud. They endeavored all they could to drown the Church in its own blood. But this opinion is not very probable because the former danger in the practices of the dragon did not comprehend this flood, and it seems clearly to be mentioned already in verse 11, where it is said, *They loved not their lives unto death.*

Others, by this flood, understand the eruption of the Franks and Vandals, Huns and Longobards who, about the year 400, broke in upon Asia and Europe like a temptest and a swelling inundation and, in a sort, overwhelmed the Christian world. This, I confess, was a flood, but whether it is that which is is implied in the text, I greatly doubt because the text speaks of a flood cast out of the mouth of the serpent. But in the eruptions of those forementioned people, there was neither the serpent nor the mouth. It was plain, public, notorious cruelty, managed by the hand, not a danger managed by secret subtlety and in the mouth.

Viegas, by this flood, understands a strange kind of Antichrist, who shall send out his army into the wilderness and, by his satellites (surely he means some pursuivants or busy emissaries) should search caves and dens to find out the faithful, whom the earth (in a literal sense) should swallow up as it did Dathan and Abiram; but this fancy is not worth the confuting. Only let me subjoin this, that some interpreters fasten this flood upon the true Antichrist of Rome, and, questionless, virtually it will reach him as to the practice; but whether it will reach the text as to its principal scope, I question.

But not to trouble you with more conjectures, the best interpreters I have met with unanimously expound this particular flood of waters to be those notorious errors, heresies, blasphemies, and schisms which Satan, by several instruments, cast out to the infection of the Church, and to the subversion of the faith immediately under the Christian emperors. When the Church of Christ obtained a little respite from the cruel sword and began to enjoy some breathing tranquility, then, all of a sudden, there broke out that flood of the Arian heresy (even in the time of Constantine the Great), wherein the Deity of the Son of God was oppugned and blasphemed. And this flood rose so high and ran so swift that, in a short time, it overwhelmed the East, and after that the West, so that, in a manner, the whole world turned Arian. After that, another flood broke out - the Macedonian heresy, opposing the Deity of the Holy Ghost.

Soon after this the Pelagian heresy, against the whole gospel; and the Nestorian and Eutychian heresy, against the verity of the Person of Christ, which floods continued upon the Church for nearly 300 years. And what mischief accrued unto the Church of Christ by every one of them, you may abundantly read in Eusebius, Socrates, Euagrius, Sozomen, Theodoret, and others.

So that now we are come, in some good measure, to perceive what this flood cast out of the mouth of the serpent is: namely, erroneous, false, wicked, heretical doctrines, cast out of the mouths of corrupt and corrupting seducers, opposing the truth and endangering the very essence or being of the Church of Christ, concerning which, favor me with your patience while I show unto you:

First, the nature of heresies and erroneous doctrines which the serpent cast out of his mouth.

Second, the danger of them to the Church of Christ, that they are perilous and hazardous.

Third, the greatness of that danger. It is the chief and the worst.

Fourth, some pertinent, useful applications of all this to us for our present humbling and reforming.

I. OF THE NATURE OF HERESIES

To find this out, you may be pleased to know that the word "heresy" admits of a three-fold signification and use.

1. Sometimes it is taken for any new and select opinion, contrary to the common and usually-received opinions of other men; in which the word "heresy" may sometimes bear a good construction, Acts 24:14, *For after that way which the Jews called heresy, did Paul worship the God of his fathers.*

2. Sometimes it is taken for any false opinion whatsoever, wherein a person recedes from any divine truth and, thereby, foments divisions, sects, and contentions.

3. But strictly among divines, it is taken for some notorious, false, and perverse opinion, opposing and subverting the faith once delivered to the saints, as Jude says, or overthrowing the form of wholesome words, as Paul says. And it may be thus described:

Heresy is an erroneous or false opinion, repugnant unto and subverting the doctrine of faith revealed in the Word as necessary unto salvation; and obstinately maintained and pertinaciously adhered unto by a professed Christian.

1) Heresy is an erroneous opinion, *falsa sententia* or *falsum dogma.* There is a difference between an evil

work and heresy. An evil work is one thing; heresy is another thing. In the work which a man does, there may be sin, very much sin, but properly there is not heresy. *Erratum* it may be, but error it is not unless it resides in the understanding.

The works of hypocrisy and of profaneness (like murder, injustice, adultery, theft, etc.) have much wickedness in them; but, unless these become the objects of opinion as well as practice, they are not heresies. Indeed if, beside the moral practice of them, anyone rises to an intellectual opinion that the practice of them is lawful and not repugnant to the Word of God, now such an opinion, erroneous opinion, of them may come to heresy.

Yea, let me add a little more. Though many practical works are acted that are repugnant to the conscience, yet the works, simply considered as works, are not to be reputed heresies. For then every sin against knowledge should be heresy. No, it is not light shining and working against an action or work which raises it to be a heresy, but it must be light in the Word shining against an opinion, which must denominate it to be heresy.

2) Heresy is an erroneous opinion concerning matters of faith. There are questions and questions (but different Greek words) as Gregory Nazianz has well distinguished. Every erroneous opinion is not heresy. To make the erroneous opinion amount to heresy, two things must concur:

One, the error must be about faith. Although a man errs in his own opinon within the proportion of *objectum scibile*, as against the rules and principles of several sciences (Geometry, Astronomy, Natural Philosophy), yet this error is not heresy; for heresy is an erroneous opinion not about matters of human science, but about matters of divine faith. But, if the error is about the matters of faith revealed in the Word, such as Christ is not God or is not Man, here now the error will rise to heresy, for here is *dogma fidei.*

Another is that the error is against faith; against the faith as well as about the faith. If it is an opinion contrary to sound doctrine, overthrowing the foundation, this will make the error to be heresy. An opinion may be contrary not only to the Church of Rome, and many particular traditions, but also to the judgment of some godly men; yet it is not, therefore, a heresy. But then it is heresy when the opinion is *contra fidem traditam,* contrary to the faith, to the doctrine of faith in the Scriptures. Nevertheless, here we must carefully consider that an opinion may be said to be contrary to the faith in a double respect:

a) One, when it is not concordant to every truth whatsoever which is revealed in the Scriptures. I dare not say that every error in this respect is heresy. There may be many mistakes, perhaps dissonant to the true chronology, to the exact and full history of some places, yet these are not necessarily heresies.

b) The other is when it is repugnant to the truth, or any truth, which is necessary to salvation, and here, no doubt, the error against faith will prove to be heresy.

There may be diverse opinions, yet none of them are heresies. In the interpretation of the Scriptures, there is frequently a variety of opinions but, as long as the lines of a circumference meet in the center, as long as every one of them unites and harbors within the analogy of faith, there is no heresy though there is some variety. But then it is heresy when the opinion is adverse, is contrary to, is subversive of, the faith revealed as necessary to salvation, which opinion may be either:

Explicitly. When the error is manifestly fundamental, it expressly plucks up the foundation. It is not a problematical canvasing of a truth, but a plain gunpowder plot, an error which blows up a fundamental truth. It does not blow off the tiles of the house, but blows up the bottoms and supports of the house, like a person who denies the Godhead of Christ, redemption by Christ, or salvation by Christ. Or it may be:

Reductively. This is when the error overthrows that which, being denied and overthrown; the foundation thereupon, and thereby, is by an inevitable necessity also denied and overthrown, or maintains that which, being maintained, a fundamental truth must necessarily and unavoidably be subverted. For example, if any person should maintain human satisfactions to be sufficient to merit and procure salvation; this error would necessarily subvert man's salvation founded upon the merits of Jesus Christ only.

3) If the erroneous opinion is against any particular doctrinally necessary truth, even that particular error will amount to heresy. Indeed, number (if I may so speak) is requisite to apostasy, but any particular necessity of a truth to our salvation (if opposed) is sufficient for heresy. The apostate turns his back from the whole truth. The heretic grapples with some truth, but denies other truth; and, therefore, though a person still retains an assent consonant to many truths, nay, to most truths, nay, to all except one necessary truth, yet,

if his erroneous opinion is subversive of that one, his error will come to heresy.

4) To make the erroneous opinion to be heretical, it is necessary (as to the person who holds it) that he be a professed Christian. It is a question put by schoolmen and others whether infidels, pagans, and Jews who hold opinions contrary unto and subversive of the faith are to be reputed heretics. Unto which I answer that one may be called heretical either:

a) Materially, like when his opinion, for the matter and substance of it, is contrary to the faith and subversive of the foundation; or else

b) Formally, when not only the substance of the opinion is heretical and opposed to the Christian faith, but also it is maintained by one who has formerly engaged himself to the profession and maintenance of the faith.

In the former consideration, infidels and Jews may be reputed heretics, but, in this latter consideration, only he is so to be reputed who was reckoned among the number of Christians professing the faith. If the infidel and Jew deny Jesus Christ to be a Savior of sinners, though this is a great sin, yet it is not (strictly considered) a heresy because neither the one nor the other ever embraced or professed the gospel. But, if a Christian professing the gospel does this, in him it is heresy.

5) But, lastly, to make up heresy, there must be obstinacy or pertinacity joined with that erroneous opinion which is contrary to the faith. He who is a heretic must adhere or inhere; he must obstinately adhere or cleave to his erroneous opinion. I confess that it is a very quick case whether pertinacity is so essential

to heresy that the opinion cannot at all be reputed heretical unless the professing Christian who holds it appears obstinate. Concerning which case, I will only deliver my opinion, submitting it to better judgments, that where the erroneous opinion appears, by natural reason, grossly and notoriously harmful to the rasing of the foundation, it is heretical. Denying Jesus Christ to be the Son of God, or denying salvation by Him, such an opinion, in the very nature of it, is pernicious, ruinous, and damnable. Yet, in the ordinary way of discovery and process with heretics, I humbly conceive that pertinacity must be an ingredient to constitute the person to be heretically erroneous.

There is *infidelis,* one who never entertained or professed the faith, yet is obstinately and most violently carried against it. This man may be a persecutor, but he is not a heretic, notwithstanding his opinion and notwithstanding his obstinacy.

Again, there is *dubius in fide,* one who is doubtful in the faith. He is one who is wavering and reeling; his anchor does not fasten; he is not quite on nor quite off, but staggers and totters. The equal apprehensions of truth and falsehood so poise and balance the one against the other that he does not come up fully and determinately any way. Now, although some affirm that doubt is heresy, I dare not assert it. Thomas the apostle doubted; he was incredulous, but not heretical. Austin says that one who doubts errs, for the man errs who approves falsehood for truth, or disallows truth for falsehood, or takes uncertain things for certain truths, or certain truths for uncertain conjectures. There is error here, but not heresy.

There is also *haeretico-credens.* This is one who is

rolled up, wriggled in, packed up into a dangerous error. He is misled, seduced, follows his leader; he holds that which is really contrary to the faith and destructive, yet not out of obstinacy of mind, but upon an imagination of truth; not out of deliberation, but by surreption. He is utterly deceived by taking upon trust. His erroneous opinion is not fortified with pertinacity, but only crept into him by his simplicity. And, therefore, being candidly dealt with and admonished, he does not contend, but yields and wheels about to the truth. As the bow, when the string is taken off, returns to its own posture again, so, upon admonition, the seduced person quits his error and submits to the faith.

But then there is the very heretic, and he is one who not only errs in his opinion, but also obstinately maintains that error. He not only holds that which is contrary to the faith, but he also holds the same with a pertinacious spirit.

But here, now, falls in that difficult and knotty question, namely, when a person is to be reputed obstinate or pertinacious in holding an error contrary to the faith. The apostle, I think, resolves us in this when he says, Titus 3:10, *A heretic after the first and second admontion, reject.* So, then, when there is a due proposal of the truth manifestly revealed in the Scriptures, and yet the erroneous person adheres to his error out of a very depravity of mind, and will not suffer his understanding to be captivated unto the truth, this person is pertinacious in holding his erroneous opinion and is manifestly a heretic.

Beloved! When an erroneous person maintains his opinion contrary to clear light so that he must necessarily deny the truth of God or revoke his error; or when he cannot maintain his wicked error, but he must necessarily overthrow some other article of faith which yet he would not do; or when the person does not care if he tramples down another truth to uphold his error against a former truth, makes one article a footstool to pull down another; or when the person steps from one error to a more gross one, and does not care what error he plunges himself into, for that he maintain his error; or when all solid reason is silenced, nay, if reason and conscience might speak, they (concurring with the truth against his error) secretly condemn him and, having nothing to reply, he falls into proud scorns, bitter virulence, miserable shifts, surely such an erroneous person is obstinate and pertinacious in his corrupt opinion.

And thus, briefly, for the first question, which contains the nature of heresies. I now come to the second particular, which respects the danger of heresies.

II. OF THE DANGER OF HERESIES

That heresies, or erroneous doctrines and opinions, are dangerous, cannot be so much as a scruple to any Christian upon the earth, unless he is turned into a heretic or into an atheist, for:

First, the Scriptures charge sin, perniciousness, and damnation upon them. St. Paul reckons up heresies among those works of the flesh which shut persons out from inheriting the kingdom of God, Galatians 5:20-21. And St. Peter calls them pernicious and damnable, and such as bring swift destruction; and, speaking of the authors of them, he says that their damnation slumbers not, 2 Peter 2:1-3.

A man's opinion makes him sinful as well as his practice; and a man may be damned for a corrupt opinion as well as for a corrupt conversation. I will not put it to a dispute whether a sin against the rule of faith may not be far more sinful and damnable than the sin which is against the rule of life. But let it suffice for the present that if heresies and heterodoxies are such sins, are such locks as can shut up the gates of heaven against a soul, if they are such bars as can break up the doors of hell and bring damnation, surely that man is not himself who doubts whether they are dangerous or not.

Second, let us consider unto what dangerous things heresies and corrupt doctrines are compared in Scripture, and by what dangerous creatures heretics and false teachers are expressed. By them you may judge whether heresies are dangerous or not.

1. Heresies are compared in Scripture sometimes to a gangrene or canker, 2 Timothy 2:17, *Their word will eat as doth a canker.* The canker is an invading ulcer, creeping from joint to joint, corrupting one part after another till, at length, it eats out the very heart and life. Sometimes they are compared to a shipwreck, 1 Timothy 1:19-20, *Hold faith and a good conscience, which some having put away concerning faith have made shipwreck.* In what a condition are the miserable passengers, when their ship is split asunder by the rock? All their goods are lost, and all their lives too. Christ calls them leaven; Paul calls them a bewitching; learned writers call them a leprosy, poison, fire, and tempest, and our text calls them a flood.

2. As for heretics, they are expressed by creatures, very dangerous and hurtful. Sometimes they are called

foxes, Song of Solomon 2:15, *The foxes which spoil the grapes.* Sometimes they are called dogs, rending dogs, Philippians 3:2, *Beware of dogs, beware of the concision.* Sometimes they are called wolves, *grievous wolves which devour the flock,* Acts 20:29. Sometimes they are called very mountebanks, cheaters, *such as beguile unstable souls.*

3. Third, Jesus Christ and His apostles give special charges and caveats agains them, to take heed and beware of them, which they never would have done had they not been dangerous. Mark 8:15, *Beware of the leaven of the Pharisees.* Matthew 7:15, *Beware of false prophets.* Matthew 24:4-5, *Take heed that no man deceive you, for many shall come in My name saying, I am Christ, and shall deceive many.* Philippians 3:2, *Beware of dogs, beware of evil workers, beware of the concision.* 2 Peter 3:17, *Beware lest ye also, being led away with the error of the wicked, fall from your own steadfastness.* Certainly, all these things clearly prove that there is a danger in them.

But that is not all. Danger is not all; there is yet more than mere danger in them, which will appear in the resolving of the third particular.

III. THE GREATNESS OF DANGER BY HERESIES

Heresies are the greatest and highest of dangers to the Church of Christ. You will imagine that the sword, prison, exile, dispersion, spoiling, torments, tortures, and the most cruel deaths which befell the Church in the primitive times were extremely dangerous, and so they were; but yet not half as dangerous as the floods of heresies and corrupt opinions are. The Church ever gained by the former, grew more in purity, in unity, in prayer, in zeal and courage. But did it ever get so by heresies and erroneous doctrines? Not unless it was by accident and after much striving and medicine for recovery.

I will go no further than the text itself to set out to you the exceeding mischief and danger which comes by heresies and erroneous doctrines. They are, in the text, called a flood cast out of the mouth of the serpent. Now, seriously consider:

1. They are a corrupting and defiling flood. Any flood is so; it presently defiles the pure waters, spoils the grounds, leaves filth and slime and mud behind it. But, surely, a flood that comes out of the mouth of a poisonous serpent is so; and there are four precious things which wicked errors or heresies poison, corrupt, and defile:

The first is the souls of men. And is there a more noble and choice thing in man, or belonging to man, than his soul? Our soul is of more value than all the world; but heresies and wicked doctrines corrupt the soul, nay, many souls. It was the heavy indictment against Babylon that *in her were found slaves and souls of men*, Revelation 18:13. Heretics, in one place, are called "merchants," *making merchandise of you with feigned words*, 2 Peter 2:3. In merchandising, there is something bought for a certain price. In this merchandise, the souls of people are bought for feigned words, for base metal, only for a corrupt error.

Every heretical opinion buys a soul or stabs a soul. It stabs the soul of him who maintains it, and still it trades on to murder more souls. It lifts off the soul from the foundation upon which the salvation of souls is built. What will become of a house whose foundation is removed? And what will become of a soul whose bottom for salvation is denied and rejeted? Damnable heresies make us to *deny the Lord that bought us,* 2 Peter 2:1. Oh, what is this! What will follow upon this, when a poor sinner comes to deny the Lord Jesus who bought him?

The second is the leading faculty of the soul. There is more danger to corrupt a captain than to corrupt many private soldiers, and most danger to corrupt a general who leads the whole army. It is capital, in some places, and at some times, to cast poison into the spring. This will poison all the streams. Heresies corrupt the great leader of the whole soul. The judgment of man is the general, the admiral, the shepherd, the overseer, the guide, the eye, the primary mover for the rest of the spheres in man. If the light in man is darkness, how great is that darkeness? If the judgment is infected, how dangerous is that infection?

Beloved! If there is the darkness of ignorance from inapprehension in the mind, the soul, hereby, is in an ill case. If there is the darkness of misapprehension by error, it is in a worse case. But when that misguiding error befalls the leading faculty of all the soul, and this error falls point-blank against a truth necessary unto the man's salvation, and, moreover, this error is stiffly adhered to by that leading judgment, it misleads and will mislead. Oh, now, in what a desperate condition is the whole soul thereby! If it does not recover from this error, it dies because of it, and it can never be recovered until the judgment is altered. And when will that judgment be altered, which perversely affronts and rejects the light of truth, which alone can carry it off?

The third is the most active faculty of the soul. They

defile and corrupt the conscience. Now, this is amazingly dangerous. A wicked error is blinding while in the judgment only, but it is binding when it slips into the conscience also. It is a wrangling Sophister in that, but it is a working Jesuit in this. Diseases falling among the vital spirits are most quick and most dangerous. Errors are never more pernicious than when they drop into the conscience, for whatever engages conscience engages all, and the utmost of our all. If the conscience of man is made a party against the truth, now all that a man has and all that a man can do will be made out against the truth too. Now, the person will, with Paul, grow mad and desperate against Christ, for Paul, being engaged by an erroneous conscience, consented to the death of Stephen. Yea, could he, in that condition, have met with Jesus Christ Himself, he would have done the same against Him.

The fourth is the conversations of men. Heresy is seldom or never divided from impiety. Hymenaeus, who made shipwreck of the faith, made shipwreck also of a good conscience. Those whom Paul called "dogs" he also called "evil workers." And, in another place, speaking of some whose minds were defiled, he adds, *and reprobate to every good work.* Our Savior, speaking of false prophets, said, *You may know them by their fruits.* The lives of men are consonant to the judgments of men. Truth and goodness are reciprocal, and so are falsehood and wickedness. The doctrine of faith is a doctrine of holiness too. And the doctrine of lies is the doctrine of profaneness too. He who falls from truth to falsehood will quickly fall from piety to wickedness. Truth is of a reforming virtue as well as of an informing nature. It salts and seasons both heart and life; but that error which putrifies the heart will putrify the life also. The plague will, at length, rise and break out into blanes and blotches.

They who write the story of the Anabaptists begin it with error in their judgments, but end it with wickedness in their practices. And Cyprian, writing long since of Novatus, that pestilent heretic, said of him that he was one who itched after a few notions, and was beyond measure covetous, intolerably proud, no man so treacherous. He would commend you before your face, but cut your throat behind your back; as false a person as ever lived, a very firebrand who did not care what became of truth or peace. He turned the world upside down so that he might carry on his opinion.

The apostle, speaking of Antichrist, calls him that man of sin, no such sinner as he. Lyranus expounds it as one totally given up to sin, and Theophylact calls him "the ringleader of sin." And truly, it is most just with God to give them up to corrupt lives who, rejecting His truth, have given up themselves to corrupt errors and lies.

2. Heresies are a drowning and overwhelming flood. A flood, you know, is such a collection, such a heightening confluence of waters, as swells the rivers above their bounds and lays all under water. Now, there are three things which heresies overwhelm.

One is the glory of all glories, the glorious name of God, the glorious name of Christ, the glorious name of the Holy Spirit, the glorious name of divine truths. Heresy turns the glory into a lie. It gives God the lie, and Christ the lie, and the Holy Spirit the lie, for it gives truth the lie, the Scriptures the lie, which are the glory of God, and Christ, and the Holy Spirit. He who makes the Word of God a liar makes God Himself a liar.

O sirs! What is God without truth? And what is all the goodness of the gospel without truth? And what is all the fabric of man's salvation without truth? Truth is, as it were, the pin, the clasp, the knot that ties all. Pull out that, untie and break that, the excellencies of God, the glories of Christ, the sweetness of the promises, the souls of men, the salvation of men's souls, all are dashed, are broken, are gone. And such work heresy makes. It dissolves the bond of all glory, yea, it resolves God into worse than nothing. No God is better than a false god. There is an open or secret blasphemy in all heresies. No man can condemn the truth of God, but in that he must likewise condemn the God of truth.

The second is the glory of religion. Religion is clipped and darkened. It grows low and beggarly when it is patched with error. It is a debasing of the gold to marry it with any metal of a courser birth. All religion is so much more excellent by how much more truth it has; but, when once it is adulterated, when once it is tainted and leavened with damnable errors, now the silver is become dross; the glory is departed from it. When a religion is like Nebuchadnezzar's image, part clay and part iron, it becomes low and contemptible. If the mixture of human inventions abates its glory, what an impairing is the mixture of corrupt, poisonous, and faith-subverting doctrines?

The third is not only the dignity, but also the very vital entity of a Church. Truth is the soul of that body, and falsehood is death unto it. Schisms do much harm, but nothing like vile doctrines. Schisms only rent the coat, but heterodoxies rent the heart. Those pluck up the fence, but these pull down the building. Those tear away the children's lace, but these bereave the children of their bread. Those are a turbulent sea; these are a dead sea. Those scratch, but these kill. Men talk much of unchurching, and of Antichrist, and the limbs of Antichrist, but a church is never more near to giving up the ghost than when it is most near to giving up the truth. It is never nearer to being unchurched, and to be essentially Antichristed, than when the truth fails, and when abominable heresies and corrupt doctrines swarm in it. Mark seriously that place in 1 John 4:3, *Every spirit that confesseth not that Christ is come in the flesh is not of God,* and this is that spirit of Antichrist. Aye, this is that spirit of Antichrist. That spirit of error and false doctrine is the spirit of Antichrist.

3. Heresies are a sudden rising flood. A flood is no sober or quiescent puddle, no grave or slow-paced river, but it is a quick and extemporary collection and inundation. And, truly, herein lies the greatness of the danger unto a people and Church by heresies. They are quickly conceived and quickly brought forth; quickly born and quickly thriving. Truth, however, gets on very slowly by reason of that incapacity of the judgment for supernaturals, and by reason of that natural opposition in man to the things of God, and by reason of the subtle interposition of the prince of darkness, who blinds the minds of men, lest the light of the glorious gospel should shine unto them.

Yet erroneous and false opinions break out with ease and spread swiftly. They are like the plague, which is a flying arrow. There needs no preparation of the ground for nettles. If the seeds merely drop down, you will soon have a full crop, yet the ground must be prepared again and again to receive good seed. The hearts of men are as naturally disposed to suck in errors as they are to send out wickednesses. The tinder is so prepared to catch the fire that it is but the striking of the flint and the work is done.

The Scriptures compare false doctrines to leaven. Oh how fast does a little leaven sour the lump! Paul wondered that the Galatians were so soon removed to another gospel, Galatians 1:6. The good man slept but one night, and the field was sown all over with tares by the wicked and envious man.

How quickly did the world turn Arian? How suddenly did the Anabaptists endanger Germany? The vines which have been some months in growing are in very few hours torn down and destroyed by foxes and wild boars.

Now, if erroneous doctrines are, in themselves, so pernicious, and in their operation so speedily diffusive, then certainly they are of all other things the most dangerous to the Church of Christ. A plague which suddenly infects many families is, therefore, the more dangerous; and heresies, which can suddenly infect many souls, are therefore the more dangerous evils.

4. Heresies are an increasing and swelling flood. A flood at first makes the river only to look big, and to run a little thicker and faster; but, after awhile, it causes the river to be unruly, to break in pieces, to superabound. The waters contribute on every side and at ever corner to raise and mount so that there is no passing. False doctrines, at first, seem to be modest. They will be but questions and queries, and then they come to be probabilites, and then they come to be tolerable conclusions, and then they rise to be unques-

tionable tenets, and then are fit to be made public articles, and then are necessary to be held, and then the contrary is not to be maintained or spoken for, nay, to be disdained and reproached.

But this is not all either; for, as false opinions rise thus, and increase in their direct line of particular magnitudes by way of intention, so they likewise enlarge themselves in divers breadths by way of extension. They are like circles in a pond. One circle begets another. So one heresy begets another; a lesser begets a greater. As one moral sin is but a stair to step down lower, so this intellectual sin of heresy is but a stair to help up to higher and worse errors.

If you will consult historical antiquity, it is wonderful to behold the great flames bred out of small sparks. What monstrous opinions have been built upon errors which seemed but little at the first. How one error has hatched a greater! They who write of them can distinctly tell us where the man was first planet-struck (what his first error was); but, after awhile, they are non-plussed in the account. The number of errors has doubled and tripled, such a maze and labyrinth is error. It is like a whirlpool which first sucks in one part and then another, and never desists until it draws in and plunges the whole body.

Besides ancient examples, we may see this swelling growth of erroneous opinions in the Church of Rome, where one error still advanced to more errors, and those again to higher errors, and these still ran on until a general corruption ensued from all the particulars. Compare the first defections and corruptions with their last and present. How little then, how total now; how particular then, how universal now. And you will easily acknowledge what increasing floods erroneous opinions are.

The points, at first, were rather about private interests of precedence, but they have so increased unto all things doctrinal that they are scarcely found in any. Their errors about the Scriptures and traditions, about the offices of Christ, about human satisfaction and merits, about invocation and adoration of saints, about justification and faith, about good works, about free-will, about the Sacraments, are evident to all the world.

I could give you an instance also in the Anabaptists in Germany, whose first author there (said David Chytraeus, in his *Dedicatory Epistle to Ericus, King of the Swedes*) was Nicolaus Pelargus Cygneus, about the year 1523. His erroneous doctrines, though bad enough, for they were laid in the contempt of the ministry of the Word and Sacraments, and rejection of the civil magistrate, yet were not formerly so numerous, but when these opinions descended unto Thomas Munzer and Andreas Carlstadt, then they began to swell both in the quantity of the opinions, and in the vast number of disciples too.

Lambertus Danaeus, in his annotations and explications of St. Augustine's book *De Haeresibus & Quod Vult Deum,* adds to that account the many derivations and enlarging propogations of heresies from age to age, showing exactly the several heresies flowing from some one capital and original heresy, as from Simon Magus's heresy, and from that of Valentinus, and that of Cardo, and that of Artemon, and that of Novatus, and that of Arius, etc. In that elaborate work of his, you may read of such a strange growth of heresies that they never stopped multiplying and breeding until they had (as much as in them lay) overthrown and cashiered every person in the Trinity: all the Scriptures, the Law and the gospel, every distinct moral commandment, every particular article of faith, every ordinance of Jesus Christ, the preaching of the Word, baptism, the Lord's Supper, etc.

There are four general heads unto which, usually, we reduce the Christian religion: (1) The Decalogue of the Law; (2) The symbol of faith; (3) The Lord's Prayer; and (4) the Sacraments. And that learned author, Danaeus, (see him in *apusc. indice terlio,* p.142, etc., printed at Geneva in folio, 1583) by name instances the several heretical, erroneous teachers who have invaded every one of these, and in every particular comprehended in them, by all which it most clearly appears how dangerously mischievous heretical opinions are to the Church of God.

5. There is one more thing which I would add in the last place, by which it shall be manifested that these heretical opinions are more dangerous than any other floods, and that is a diverse quality in them. Other floods are quickly up and quickly down. Although they grown high and perilous, there is a sudden transiency in the height and peril. Their principles are unconstant though violent and, being spent, these ordinary floods sink and famish for want of supply and feeding. But the floods of false and erroneous doctrines are such as quickly rise, but very slowly abate. They are, in this respect, worse than the great deluge in the days of Noah, which continued many months, but then slacked and sank, and fell quite away.

It is not so with heretical errors; they are like diseases which come upon us flying, but go away from us creeping. Some erroneous opinions have been kept up for forty years together, nay, above one hundred years together, some of them for three hundred years.

Oh, brethren! Men dote upon their own fancies; they are exceedingly pleased with their own brats, especially with the new concepts of their own minds. They dearly like them, love them, and foster them. For one heretic who has been poisoned in his judicials, you will find a thousand others converted and reduced who have only been stained in their morals. Heresy, or the heretical opinion, is styled up by all the parts, arguments, shifts, learning of carnal reason, and it is born up by a haughty, disdainful, and proud spirit. And it is so fallacious and fraudulent, when you come to handle it, and it is so rammed in with obstinance and peremptoriness, that it is almost a miracle to work effectually upon a heretic.

Every heretic is odiously proud. All other men who dissent from him are far below him, and one said very truly, "No proud man can endure to be accounted a fool or a knave." So simple as to be deceived or so base as to deceive, one of which the heretic thinks he must take to his share if at any time he recants his heretical and seducing doctrine.

I should now come to show unto you the reasons why Satan makes use of this dangerous flood against the Church, and why especially at some times more than others. He well knows that there remains in professing Christians many advantages for him as to erroneous opinions, much ignorance, much pride and self-conceitedness, much itching vanity, much vain glory, much faternal envy, much carelessness and inadvertency, etc., but I must wave this and conclude all with some seasonable applications unto ourselves.

APPLICATION

USE 1. Are heresies, erroneous and false doctrines, such a dangerous and pernicious flood to the Church of God? Is there so much sinfulness in them? So much dishonor to Christ? So much injury to the truth of God? So much hazard to the immortal souls of men? Oh, then, what just, what sad, what singular cause do all of us have this day to enlarge our tears and humiliations? There are many floods which call for our tears: the flood of innocent blood in Ireland; the flood of cries from poor widows and orphans; the flood of needy and wounded soldiers, and there is yet another flood, a worse flood, the flood of heresies and blasphemies. One deep calls for another, the flood of wicked and ungodly opinions calls earnestly for a flood of sorrow and lamentation.

We are, by God's mercy and goodness, indifferently rescued from the cruelty of dragons. Oh, but now we are as much endangered with the flood of the serpent! The bodies of people are, in some good measure, secured from the edge of the sword; but what of this while the souls of people are hazarded with the poison of errors? If the danger flies from the body to the soul, if the corporal danger is exchanged for a spiritual danger, where is our happiness? What is our safety by this?

Beloved, there are four notable reasons for our most solemn humiliation for the spiritual wickednesses, for the false and abominable doctrines which, like a flood, are now overwhelming this nation.

I. The account or height of some of them. They amount to no less than execrable blasphemies, to ignominious, contemptuous, disgraceful reproaches of God, Christ, and the Holy Scriptures. Believe me, blasphemy is a daring sin. It presses very close and too sore upon God. *He that blasphemeth the name of the Lord, he shall surely be put to death,* Leviticus 24:16. The words according to the original are, "He that strikes through the name of Jehovah." Blasphemy is that bold sword which is hacking God Himself, which is, as it were, cleaving of Him asunder. The schoolmen tell us that blasphemy breaks out in three ways.

First, when we affirm that of God which is unbecoming of God, which is incompatible with His holy and divine nature; as to make Him a creature, a liar, or to make Him cruel, unjust, unmerciful, sinful, or the cause of sin.

Second is when we deny that to God which indeed belongs to God. It is called blasphemy in the king of Assyria when he said that *the Lord was not able to deliver Jerusalem out of his hand,* 2 Chronicles 32:17.

Third is when we put that upon the creature which is proper to God. Thus, when the Israelites had made a molten calf and said, *This is thy God that brought thee up out of Egypt,* it is added that they brought great provocations, Nehemiah 9:18. In the Hebrew it is, "And they committed great blasphemies."

Now, compare this short discourse of the kinds of blasphemies with the many expressions let fall in the speeches of some, and set down in the writings of others, and then judge whether some of our modern errors do not rise as high as blasphemy.

1. That God is the author of sin; not only of the actions unto which sin cleaves, but of the very sinfulness itself: of the disorderliness, depravity, and irregularity.
2. That the saints in this life are fully perfect, as omnisicient as God.
3. That the fullness of the Godhead dwells bodily in every saint in the same measure as it did in Christ Jesus while He was here on earth.
4. That when the fullness of the Godhead shall be manifested in the saints, then they shall have more power than Christ had, and do greater works than He did, and that they shall then have divine honor.
5. And one has been complained of for saying that Jesus Christ was a bastard.
6. Another said that he was Jesus Christ, the Messiah.
7. That Jesus Christ is not God essentially, but nominally.
8. That His human nature was defiled with original sin like ours.
9. That He is not of a holier nature than men.
10. That it is as possible for Jesus Christ to sin as it is for a child of God to sin.
11. That there is no such thing as the Trinity of Persons.
12. That the Scriptures are but of human invention, a mere shadow, a false history, and ought not to be the foundation of any man's faith any more than the Apocrypha and other books, etc.

When Hezekiah heard the blasphemies of Rab-shakeh, he rent his clothes, covered himself with sack-cloth, went into the house of the Lord, and sent to the prophet Isaiah, saying, *This is a day of trouble, and of rebuke, and of blasphemy.* That day of blasphemy was a day of trouble and vexation to him. Though the blasphemy was from an Assyrian, yet it was a day of trouble to him. And what should the day be unto us when it is a day of many blasphemies, and that not from professed Assyrians, but from professing Christians? What Christian can hear, can bear, such indignities and reproaches cast upon his God and his Christ without a bleeding and rising spirit?

II. The breadth or number of false and erroneous opinions. So many and so grievous! Verily, they grow so thick, so abundant, that they will leave us neither Church nor state, neither minstry nor ordinances, neither duties nor worship. There are some who have printed large catalogues of them; I will but pick a few of the more notorious of them and spread them before you this day.

1. The Scriptures of the Old Testament do not bind us Christians, nor those of the New Testament either, any further than the Spirit (for the present) reveals unto us that such a place is the Word of God.
2. That God never loved one man more than another before the world, and that the decrees are all conditional.
3. That there is no original sin.
4. That the will of man is still free, even to supernaturals.

5. That the saints may fall totally and finally from grace.
6. That Christ died alike for all, yea, that the salvific virtue of His death extends to all reprobates as well as to the elect, yea, to the very devils as well as unto men.
7. That Jesus Christ came into the world not for satisfaction, but for publication; not to procure for us, and unto us, the love of God, but only to be a glorious Publisher of the gospel.
8. That God is not displeased at all if His children sin, and it is no less than blasphemy for a child of God to ask pardon for his sins.
9. That sanctification is a dirty and dungy qualification.
10. That the doctrine of repentance is a soul-destroying doctrine.
11. That fastings and humblings are legal and abominable.
12. That the souls of men are not immortal but mortal.
13. That there is no heaven to crown the godly and no hell to torment the ungodly.
14. That civil magistracy is anti-Christian, and but a usurpation.
15. That the whole ministry of the land, as to their present ordination and standing is anti-Christian.
16. That it is as lawful to baptize cats and dogs and horses (which some have done for some of them, if not for all and more) as it is to baptize the infants of believers.
17. That there is no true ministry this day in all

the world, nor was since the general apostasy which, they say, began since the death of the last of the Apostles.

18. That there will be no ministry either until some apostles are raised up and sent; and, when those apostles come, then there will be true evangelists also, and pastors, and not until then. Hearken, O people, and judge, O Christians, whether the serpent has not cast out his flood among us! Judge whether the errors in our times do not call for more high thoughts and more deep tears.

III. The length or peril by all these. If the peril were confined only to the souls of them who are the craftsmen and founders of these opinions, yet even this should move us to lament; but the flood is running, the water is spreading. The plague is not only begun but wasting; the contagion grows to be general. It has gotten into the city, into the country, it has gotten into that (other) chief university. The poison is dropped into the springs. It has gotten into many leaders of the people who themselves err, and cause others to err. It breaths; it walks, and rolls up and down. It is spreading over the whole kingdom. It surprises place after place, infects family after family. The sword of late was not so swift to conquer bodies, as errors are now to poison souls.

Truly, sirs! If blasphemies against God; if reproaches against Christ; if decisions against the Holy Ghost; if contempt of the Scriptures; if vilifying of the ordinances of Christ; if abuses to our holy profession; if the eternal hazard of souls; if all of these cannot affect or afflict us, I do not know what to say unto you!

IV. The special engagements which are upon us all to lay all these things with sorrow to our hearts. Beloved! We are Christians (let others think of us as they please); we are covenanting Christians (let others deride this as they will); and we are, or should be, penitent Christians (let others be what they please) now.

Consider us as Christians. We take ourselves to be the children of the true and living God and profess ourselves to be the members of Jesus Christ. The faith of Christ is delivered unto us. We are entrusted with it; we are responsible for it; we are to be zealous for it. How, then, can we suffer our God, our Christ, our faith, to be thus dishonorably injured and abused, and not be troubled at all!

Consider us as covenanting Christians. So we have, every one of us, bound our souls to God. Can any mortal creature here release us? We have lifted up our hands to the Most High God in our several places to extirpate heresies and false doctrines.

Yea, consider us as penitent Christians. Fasting Christians should be so; they should be mourning Christians. And Christians who penitentially mourn will mourn for the sins of others as well as for their own sins. And they will mourn most when God is dishonored most. And can God be dishonored more than by blasphemies and damnable heresies? Put all of these together, and then consider whether these sins of heresies and blasphemies should not wound our souls with grief, which have wounded our God with so much dishonor.

USE 2. But I pass from this use of humiliation to a

second use, which shall be for exhortation, and it is this: Since there is such a flood cast out of the mouth of the serpent to carry away the woman, let us carefully improve the following words in the text, *And the earth helped the woman, and opened her mouth to swallow up the flood.* Before I distribute my exhortation, let me premise a distinction or two.

There is a two-fold opening of the mouth concerning this flood. One is to speak for damnable errors and opinions, and such as vent and maintain them. Oh, that the mouth of any Christian should ever open itself on behalf of those who dare open their mouths in blasphemy against their God and Christ! Should the welfare of a corrupt and poisonous seducer be dearer to you than the glory of your God, than the truth of your Savior?

But there is another opening of the mouth, and that is against damnable errors and heresies. We can do nothing against the truth, but for the truth, said Paul. *Contend earnestly for the faith once delievered to the saints,* said Jude. *Hold fast the faithful Word, for there are many unruly and vain talkers and deceivers, whose mouths must be stopped, who subvert whole houses, etc.,* so says the apostle in Titus 1:9-11.

Again, there is a two-fold swallowing up of this flood. One is by way of impression and furtherance, of imitation and countenance. Like the fish that swallows the bait, too many swallow up the flood in this sense: *The prophets prophesy falsely, and my people love to have it so,* Jeremiah 5:31. *There shall be false teachers, who privily shall bring in damnable heresies, and many shall follow their pernicious ways,* 2 Peter 2:1-2.

Another is by way of hindrance and repression, so

as to make the danger of this flood to sink and cease. Oh, bring in your help! Bring it in fully; bring it in speedily thus to swallow up this flood. Believe it; if you do not carefully swallow up this flood, this flood will, ere long, swallow you up, and this kingdom too.

Now, there are two sorts of men especially who may help, and who ought to help swallow up and repress the present flood of heresies and blasphemies.

1. You, right honorable men, and the rest who are Christian magistrates. It was but the scornful speech of Tiberius that the gods alone must remedy the injuries offered to them. Oh no! You are guardians of each table of the law. You are designed to be the nursing fathers. You have received the sword to be a terror to evil. Pious and learned William Ames, speaking to the question as to whether heretics are to be punished by the civil magistrate, answered thus, "The position and duty of the magistrate demands that he repress shameless disturbers with the sword, or by public external power if there is need." It is his place and duty to repress and restrain them if they are noxious and turbulent. Yea, and he adds, more than every one will be patient to hear; namely, that if also they are manifestly blasphemous and pertinacious, they may be cut off by capital punishment, according to Levitcus 24:15-16. But I will not fall upon the discussion of this at this time. All that I would humbly suggest to you is this, that you may help against the dangerous flood nine ways.

1) By a peremptory abhorring and crushing of that flood-begetting maxim, viz. a catholic liberty and toleration of all opinions. There was a religion (as one spoke before you) of all gods among the old Romans,

and there is a religion of all saints now among the Papists. And, if the serpent could but wriggle in a religion of all opinions among the English, he needs to desire no more. If men can step from one religion on to all, they will soon fall from all religion to none.

2) By a public declaration against all heresies and blasphemies known to be spoken and printed. When Ostorodius and Vaidovius started out their Socinian heterodoxies in the low countries, the States General packed away those seducers with exile, and publically condemned and committed their pestiferous books to the fire.

3) By making some standing laws against such opinions, which can be proved to be heretical and blasphemous. One has said, "Kings of the earth serve Christ also by passing laws in Christ's interest."

4) By setting up your church discipline with full power, so that it may reach these heresies and blasphemies, which, if any sins, then they plainly fall within the verge of it. If the discipline were fully and generally established, you should not have a heresy or blasphemy or any erroneous opinion creeping out in any part of the kingdom, but there would be a timely discovery of it; and, likewise, a spiritual remedy to recover erring persons and to prevent their further spreading.

5) By encouraging and heartening the godly, orthodox, painful ministers of the gospel in their assertings and vindicatings of the truths of God, and in their oppugning of wicked, dangerous, and damnable opinions; not suffering the ministers to be snibbed, abused, reviled, scorned, slandered, disturbed, or hazarded because they oppose the adversaries of truth,

and those serpents which cast out floods among us. Why should the shepherd be discouraged because he keeps wolves from the sheep? Or why should any man be checked because he would quench the flying fire?

6) By using your prudent authority in a timely causing of faithful and able ministers to be sent forth; such as are thoroughly tried and well-approved to be sound in the faith, and skillful to convince gainsayers and seducers. The more you help truth, and the servants of truth, the more help you therein contribute against errors and the enemies of truth. There is no better help against darkness than light.

7) By a tender and watchful eye unto the universities, one of which is lately fallen into your possession. Take care that it does not fall into the possession of any seducers. You have heard, no doubt, of a late disputation in Oxford where somebody undertook to maintain (besides in private) divers strange and dangerous opinions in public. I humbly entreat you to take care that the serpent does not get in his body before there is any planted to bruise his head. Truth by right is the first-born, and should inherit first. Do not put the truth to play an after-game with error. Other garrisons, if lost, may easily be reduced, but that which is surpised fast by error is not so easily recovered.

8) By enjoining a solemn day of humiliation through all the land for the dishonors redounding to God, Christ, and the truth, by the present errors, heresies, and blasphemies. Lately, you did so for the floods of rain which endangered the corn. Oh, that it might seem good unto you to do so for the flood of errors which endanger souls! This humble request I presume to leave with your pious zeal and prudence.

9) By using your coercive power with such methods and proportions as the real safety of truth and souls requires, and the repression of dangerous errors needs. So managing the distributions thereof that, under the notion of restraining heresy, you by no means injure real sanctity, nor yet, under the pretence of sanctity, you do not favor the growth of heresy. Oh, what a happy people are they among whom errors are losing and truths are gaining! Where piety thrives and wickedness blasts! Where all who are good can join against all that is evil and, in lesser things, whereas yet they cannot (through weakness) clasp opinions; yet (for the truth and peace's sake) can clasp hearts and hands to promote God's glory and the common salvation of souls!

2. I have a word also to say unto you who are ministers of the gospel of Christ. Come forth from your long silences, neglects, and reserves. Help the Church of Christ in swallowing up the flood which the serpent has cast out of his mouth. "When Jesus Christ is blasphemed, it is not a time to fear, but to cry out!" said Luther to Staupitius. Men will say that you are moderate and discreet, but what will Christ say to you, if at such a time you are silent in His cause?

Oh, my brethren! You are the husbandmen; take heed that no one sows tares in the field while you sleep. You are the builders; oh, be sure to preserve the foundation safe! You are the shepherds of the flock; oh beware of the wolves lest they break in and destroy the sheep! You are the vinedressers and keepers of the vineyard; oh, have an eye to the foxes who will otherwise spoil the tender grapes! You are the stewards of Christ; oh, be vigilant on what provision the household feeds! You are the watchmen; oh, look out lest the enemy slip in and surprise the city! You are the fathers; be sure that your children do not have a stone given to them instead of bread, or a serpent instead of a fish.

You must help with your most fervent prayers, as Alexander once did and prevailed against Arius. You must help with your counsels, with your watchings, with your preachings. You must *bona docere & mala dedocere,* as Austin says. You must stand for truth and withstand errors. You are, in a singular manner, entrusted with truth and souls. Oh, watch! Oh, pray! Oh, preach! Oh, do all that faithful ministers should do when a flood breaks in!

You read of Elijah's zeal against the false prophets, and Paul's zeal against false apostles. You have read of the zeal of Athanasius against the Arians, and of the zeal of Cyprian against the Novatians, and of the zeal of Austin against the Donatists, the Manichees, and the Pelagians. You have read of the zeal of Jerome, of Chrysostom, of Nazianzen, and many others in ancient times. You have read of the zeal of Luther and Calvin, and others in later times. You have showed your zeal to the kingdom in dangerous times.

I say no more. Remember your first works; remember your engagements, and be zealous. If you who are the angels of Christ, the ministers of Christ, the stewards of Christ, if you are drowsy, if you are silent, if you stop your own mouths when mouths are opened against Christ, whose mouth can we expect should open itself to swallow up the flood? It was a brave answer which Cyril gave to Theodosius that, in our private and personal injuries, we should hold our peace; but, when the truth (or faith) is in danger of being corrupted, we ought to speak, else we must give an account to God of our unseasonable silence.

USE 3. I have one use more. Has the serpent cast out such such a flood of errors and false doctrines among us?

1. Then let every one take heed lest he be carried away with any part of this flood. I say, take heed; for erroneous times are trying times and proving times as well as bloody and persecuting times. God has tried your fidelity to this kingdom of late by a flood of blood, and God is now trying your fidelity to the kingdom of His dear Son by a flood of errors. Take heed lest you be carried away by this flood.

There are seven things which are very apt to be carried away by a flood: light things, loose things, weak things, low things, rotten things, tottering things, and venturous things. Oh, take heed:

1) That you are not light or proud Christians. Errors are most apt to breed in a proud brain and a graceless heart; and no man is more likely to be overturned by error than he who has overturned himself by pride. The proud and blasphemers are joined together, 2 Timothy 3:2. The proud man is exposed to most temptations, to most falls, and to most errors. It is the proud man who does not consent to wholesome words of Christ, but dotes about questions, 1 Timothy 6:3-4.

2) That you are not loose Christians. If ungodliness is in the heart, it will not be hard for error to get into the head. A loose heart can best comply with loose principles. Truth is searching and reforming, but error is more quiet and gratifying. It is grace which settles the mind and establishes the heart.

3) That you are not weak Christians. Weak stomachs are most longing. A Christian whose faith is implicit and leaning on man often trusts out his judgment and soul. The weaker light you have of truth, the more easily you may be cheated with errors instead of truth.

4) That you are not low Christians. A worldly heart is a very low heart. It is, of all others, the cheapest. It will be bought and sold upon every turn to serve its own turn. The truth can never be sure in that chest which any error with a little golden key can pick. If you are the servant of truth for gain, you will be a slave to error for more gain.

5) That you are not rotten or hypocritical Christians. They were given up to believe lies who did not receive the truth in the love of it. How just is it with God, that he should fall into real error whose heart never loved real truth? That the deceitful heart should at length be a deceived heart? Is it difficult to set him against the faith who never had a sound faith?

6) Take heed that you are not tottering and unstable Christians. When the judgment is not balanced and solidly fixed upon the truths of Christ, but reeling and wavering and, like those in Elijah's time, halting between two opinions, it is usually in danger to be poised with error. He whose mind is but indifferent about a truth is more than half on his way to error.

7) Take heed that you are not venturous or soul-tempting Christians. Julian sipped in his apostasy by going to hear Libanius. The devil is ready enough to tempt you; do not be forward to tempt him. Eve lost all by hearing one sermon from the mouth of the serpent. If you will be trading among cheaters, it is no wonder if

you are cheated. We are sure to go by the worst when we venture upon our own strength. The man who exposes himself to hear new truths oftentimes comes back with old errors newly dressed.

2. Let everyone strengthen his soul that he may stand and withstand, and not be carried away. The house built upon the rock stood when the flood came. Take all in a word: A judgment solidly principled, a heart sincerely renewed, a faith truly bottomed, truth and love of it cordially matched; profession and practice well-joined, a fear of ourselves and dependence upon God still maintained, God's ordinances and the society of humble and growing Christians still frequented, watchfulness and prayer still continued are the best directives that I can deliver to keep us in the truth, and the best preservatives that I know to keep us from error.

FINIS